DEDICATED TO
The Lubavitcher Rebbe
FOUNDER OF THE CANDLE LIGHTING CAMPAIGN

*The more candles lit around the world, the more light,
for even "a little light dispels a great deal of darkness."*
-The Rebbe

IN HONOR OF ALL OUR MOTHERS
WHO PASS ON THE FLAME OF JUDAISM

IN HONOR OF ALL JEWISH WOMEN AND GIRLS
ACROSS THE GLOBE WHO LIGHT SHABBOS CANDLES

*The net proceeds of this book will be used to support
and connect our Jewish daughters around the world.*

*You are already a part of the beautiful global community of Jewish daughters!
We welcome YOU to connect with us and with each other at Jewish Girls Unite!*

TABLE OF CONTENTS

INTRODUCTION

Foreword	6
Backstory: How This Book Began	8
The Beginnings: The Bat Mitzvah	11
The Blessing Stands the Test of Time	14
Jewish Girls Unite	16
Song: One More Light	18
Complete the Circle	20
Shabbos Candle Lighting Guide	22
Time to Reflect: Connecting to the True You	25

CHAPTER 1:
Invite to Light

Story: The Power of One More Light	28
Tributes	30
Song: Are You Jewish?	34
Global Voices: Sharing the Mitzvah of Shabbos Candles	35
Time to Reflect: Share Your Light	42
Questions to Consider	42

CHAPTER 2:
A Time to Pray

Story: Creating My Own Prayer Space	44
Tributes	46
Song: I Used to Think My Mother Was the Shabbos Queen	50
Song: Miracles Go On	51
Global Voices: Personal Prayers	52
Time to Reflect: Your Prayer	58
Questions to Consider	58

CHAPTER 3:
Light Up Your Soul

Story: A Candle Ignited My Soul	60
Tributes	62
Song: Shine Your Inner Light	66
Global Voices: Shabbos Candles Light Up Our Soul	67
Time to Reflect: Your Jewish Soul Shining Brightly	75
Questions to Consider	76

CHAPTER 4:
Illuminating the Home

Story: No One is Too Small to Light Up the World	78
Tributes	81
Song: As the Sun is Setting Low	84
Song: Our Humble Home	84
Global Voices: Welcoming the Shabbos Queen	85
Time to Reflect: Welcome the Shabbos Queen	97
Questions to Consider	98

CHAPTER 5:
Transforming the Darkness

Story: Longing for the Light	100
Tributes	103
Song: Shine a Little Light	106
Song: Women of the Future	107
Global Voices: From Darkness to Light	108
A Legacy of Light: Thalia Hakin	118
Time to Reflect: The Divine Light	120
Time to Reflect: *Hashem* is My Light	121
Questions to Consider	122

CHAPTER 6:
Light of Jewish Women Past, Present & Future

Story: Reconnecting to My Roots	124
Tributes	126
Song: Let's Get Glowing	130
Song: *Letaken Olam*	131
Global Voices: Connecting Women from Generation to Generation	132
Time to Reflect: Your Precious Legacy	145
Questions to Consider	146

CHAPTER 7:
Light of Peace & Redemption

Story: My Personal Redemption	148
Tributes	150
Song: *Ani Maamin*	154
Song: My Lights	155
Global Voices: The Peace and Serenity of Shabbos	156
Time to Reflect: A World of Peace and Harmony	164
Questions to Consider	165

APPENDIX

Glossary	166
Blessings for Holidays	168
Acknowledgments	169

FOREWORD

Dear Reader,

We welcome you to open this book at the end of a long and tiring week, to pause and gaze at the beautiful pictures and inspiring words about *Shabbos* candles by Jewish girls and women around the globe. Take time to breathe and remember that G-d is your greatest and infinite source of strength, love and light. When you lovingly perform the **mitzvah of lighting your candles**, feel the glow of peace surrounding you. A little light dispels the darkness. All is well!

At Jewish Girls Unite (JGU), we are working together to connect Jewish girls of all backgrounds and empower them to shine their inner light (express creativity, love *Hashem*, and grow as leaders) in a safe online community. At special times, many of us join together in person for seasonal retreats, as well. (One of our future goals is to have a space where we can host frequent Shabbos retreats.) Using the global JGU platform, we announced a Shabbos Candle Lighting Writing Contest to create a space for Jewish girls to express their thoughts and feelings about candle lighting.

We received hundreds of thoughtful submissions from creative and talented girls across the globe. This book includes a selection of poems and stories from the contest, along with personal reflections, songs, and questions to consider. We hope they will inspire you to recognize your privilege to be an ambassador of light.

We thank all the girls, educators and mothers who submitted essays to the contest. We thank our JGU Global Leadership Team for supporting and sharing their skills and resources with our Jewish daughters. Together we are creating the Jewish mothers of tomorrow, lighting the flames today to ensure the continuity of our nation.

> *Together we are creating the Jewish mothers of tomorrow, lighting the flames today to ensure the continuity of our nation.*

We are profoundly grateful to all those who created a Legacy or Tribute Page. Thank you for sharing your loved ones with us — they will be remembered for generations. Through your tributes, you are supporting our Jewish daughters all over the world as, with your help, JGU continues to carry out its mission and broaden and deepen its impact. Thank you for ensuring that our Jewish daughters will have the tools to carry on the precious legacies of our matriarchs and keep the flame of Judaism burning for eternity!

We encourage you to use this book weekly to stir your love for *Hashem* and your feelings of being connected to all the millions of Jewish daughters around the world... After all, each and every Jewish woman is a Jewish daughter, a *Bas Yisroel*! We hope this book, *One More Light*, will inspire the inner peace and calm of Shabbos in your mind and heart. Once you feel this sense of Shabbos peace, we encourage you to allow the tranquil, soothing Shabbos atmosphere to permeate your life.

We hope this book will be used lovingly by all women and girls, for many generations to come. We hope it will help you to grow continually in your appreciation for candle lighting for the blessing it is, a privilege entrusted to women and girls every Friday eve.

Your Shabbos candles prepare the world for a time when peace and harmony will reign for eternity. Each and every Shabbos is a taste of that wonderful world of perfection, when it will be Shabbos forever. This harmonious and joyful world is what we wish for you, our dear Jewish daughters!

With love and appreciation,

Nechama Dina Laber
JGU Global Director

Susan Axelrod
JGU Global Strategy Advisor

For more inspiration, join online workshops for women and girls at www.JewishGirlsUnite.com/programs.

We invite YOU to share your thoughts, feelings, candle lighting or legacy stories at www.JewishGirlsUnite.com. Contest submissions are also on the JGU website.

BACKSTORY: HOW THIS BOOK BEGAN

The first two Candle Lighting Books published in 1977 and 1979

One More Light was inspired by the first two candle lighting books entitled *A Candle of My Own*, published by the Lubavitch Women's Organization Candle Lighting *Neshek* Campaign in the late 1970s. Rabbi Menachem Mendel Schneerson, the seventh Lubavitcher Rebbe encouraged these publications to inspire Jewish mothers and girls from the age of three (or younger) to light Shabbos candles. The books have been cherished in many homes for decades.

These publications were part of the Candle Lighting *Neshek* Campaign launched in September 1974/5734 by the Rebbe. The Rebbe named the Campaign "*Neshek*" because it is the Hebrew acronym for "*Neiros Shabbos Kodesh*," which means "candles of the holy Shabbos." "*Neshek*" also means weapon in Hebrew and reminds us that we have the power to conquer spiritual darkness with the light of Shabbos candles. He said, "We are living in a world of spiritual darkness and when Jewish girls as young as three make a blessing over a physical candle, they are bringing spiritual light into the world. The call of *Neshek* must reach even the remotest corners of the globe so young Jewish girls the world over will insist that their parents provide them with candles for lighting before Shabbos."

At the time the Rebbe also said, "No one knows what might happen in a half-hour or in an hour, and people walk around worried about what tomorrow may bring. They are forgetting that the Protector of Israel neither slumbers nor sleeps. The solution is the light of a young girl's candle, a special power bestowed upon her by Hashem to literally illuminate the world both spiritually and, as a result of the act of lighting the Shabbos candles, physically as well."

Mrs. Esther Sternberg, director of the Candle Lighting Campaign, received personal instruction from the Rebbe to publicize the call of *Neshek* throughout the world. In 1977, she received essays by young girls about Shabbos candle lighting from teachers in a Hebrew school, which she then sent to the Rebbe. The Rebbe requested that they be published in a book with color, so people can see how much children enjoy lighting candles. The first Candle Lighting Writing Contest was announced and reached girls from all backgrounds, according to the Rebbe's instructions. This led to the publication of *A Candle of My Own*, which included illustrations by artist Michoel Muchnik.

In 1979, Mrs. Esther Sternberg was a young mother, who was suddenly confined to a wheelchair due to temporary paralysis. There is a verse in Psalm 119:105 that says, "Your words of Torah guide me like a candle unto my feet (to prevent my feet from injury), and are a light for my path." Inspired by this verse, she announced a Candle Lighting Writing Contest and notified the Rebbe of the contest (together with a request for a blessing for good health). At that time, she didn't think about publishing a second book. Mrs. Sternberg recovered shortly after the successful writing contest.

Soon afterward, Mrs. Sternberg's husband received a call from the Lubavitcher Rebbe's office: "Publish the second book – even before Rosh Hashanah." This was five weeks before the High Holidays, not leaving much time for publication. The book was indeed published before Rosh Hashanah, and the Rebbe received the first copy of the book. He responded with gratitude and satisfaction.

Amazingly, the second candle lighting book includes a photo of Nechama Dina Laber, at age five.

The second book includes a collection of essays by Jewish girls from around the world, alongside beautiful photographs of girls lighting Shabbos candles, by photographer Schneur Zalman Stern. Amazingly, the second candle lighting book includes a photo of Nechama Dina Laber, at age five.

Thirty-six years later, in August 2015, Nechama Dina Laber met with Mrs. Esther Sternberg and told her that Jewish Girls Unite would like to support the work of the Candle Lighting *Neshek* Campaign to help perpetuate the Rebbe's vision. With her guidance and blessing, JGU announced a new Shabbos Candle Lighting Writing Contest for girls around the globe in September. JGU honored Mrs. Esther Sternberg with the first JGU Jewish Matriarch Award at the Global JGU Anniversary Celebration on March 15, 2016. The following year, the third candle lighting book, *One More Light*, was launched on March 1, 2017 at a Global JGU Celebration at the Jewish Children's Museum.

Mrs. Esther Sternberg, who for over 40 years has ably led the vital Candle Lighting *Neshek* Campaign, said, "We see the Rebbe had a vision that publishing the books would continue to inspire girls to light Shabbos candles and keep Shabbos. It would show people the effect that Shabbos candles have on children, and it would inspire mothers to light with their daughters, and educators to encourage their students to light Shabbos candles.

"I want to thank Jewish Girls Unite for launching the One More Light Campaign to perpetuate the Rebbe's vision. This is exactly what the Rebbe wanted. One More Light means that every person who lights one more candle will cause another person to light one more candle, and this will cause another person to light one more candle, which will bring us to the time of the redemption through the coming of *Moshiach* now."

Mrs. Esther Sternberg and her family at the 2016 Global JGU Anniversary Celebration

THE BEGINNINGS:
THE BAT MITZVAH

by Dena Fox
August 17, 2001 - 28 Av, 5761
Reprinted from the L'Chaim Magazine

This story began 22 years ago. Twelve-year-old Amy Israel was a sixth grader at the Hebrew Academy of the Capital District. She had been asked to write a poem about Shabbat and to submit it to a special project that was underway.

What had prompted the request for the poems was a book that was to be published by the Shabbat Candle Lighting Campaign of the Lubavitch Women's Organization. Initiated by the Rebbe in 1974, the Campaign had flourished under the directorship of Mrs. Esther Sternberg. The book Mrs. Sternberg undertook to publish would be entitled, *A Candle of My Own* and would contain original poems and compositions by Jewish girls from around the world.

Over the years Amy became more and more involved in Jewish observance with the help of Rabbi Yisroel and Rochel Rubin, the Rebbe's emissaries to Albany. Amy now went by her Jewish name, Emunah. She married Ron Sohn, and they had four children. Eventually, the Sohns moved to New Jersey.

When her eldest daughter, Eliana, neared her twelfth birthday, Emunah asked how she would like to celebrate this special event. Suggesting that perhaps a trip to Israel would be meaningful, Emunah was taken aback by Eliana's response.

"Oh Mom, no big party," Eliana replied. "I'll just take a couple of friends to Disney World."

Emunah was surprised that a trip to Disney World was her daughter's idea of what would be an appropriate way of celebrating becoming an adult in Judaism. Although Eliana attended a Jewish day school, Emunah realized that she needed to supplement her daughter's education in this area.

And so, Emunah phoned Nechama Laber who, together with her husband Rabbi Avraham Laber, is one of the Rebbe's emissaries in Upstate New York. Nechama had been Eliana's teacher at the Maimonides Day School when the Sohns lived in Albany.

Emunah knew that Nechama Dina had organized a Bat Mitzvah Club for girls in fifth and sixth grades to help them learn about the special journey they were about to embark upon as young Jewish women. In fact, each year Nechama Dina would ask Emunah to speak with the pre-teens about such diverse topics as cultivating friendships, maintaining relationships, and even hygiene. Emunah had seen the club from the inside out and was sure that if her daughter would be a part of the Bat Mitzvah Club experience she would grow and mature as a young Jewish woman.

"Are you still running a program for Bat Mitzvah-age girls?" Emunah asked Nechama. Nechama explained that for various reasons she had not intended to run the club that year. Emunah offered to sponsor the first club meeting at her mother's home in Albany and Nechama agreed to undertake organizing the club.

The Bat Mitzvah Club was publicized at Maimonides Day School and at the Hebrew Academy of the Capital District. Emunah and

The first Bat Mitzvah Club meeting in 2001. Eliana Sohn is the third from left.

Nechama Dina had expected about eight girls to attend the initial meeting and were delighted when 20 girls showed up from all walks of Jewish life. Thus began a monthly two-hour journey for Emunah and her daughter Eliana from New Jersey to Troy. And the relationship between Emunah and Nechama that had begun years earlier deepened.

The end of the school year was fast approaching. Nechama Laber called Emunah and asked her to speak at the special banquet that was being organized for all of the girls who had participated in the Bat Mitzvah Club, together with their mothers and grandmothers.

"A number of girls will be reading original poems," Nechama Dina informed Emunah.

"And we'd like you to speak at the banquet as well."

"Poems?" Emunah asked. Emunah recalled a conversation she'd had with Nechama a few years earlier. Nechama had been looking through a copy of *A Candle of My Own* and had noticed a poem written by Amy Israel of the Hebrew Academy of Albany. That was when Emunah had discovered that the poem she had written when she was her daughter's age was published in the book.

"Do you have a copy of *A Candle of My Own* so you can read me my poem?" she asked.

Nechama found the book and read the poem to Emunah, who had not heard the poem in 22 years. Then Emunah heard the page of the book turn and Nechama gasped in delight. On the very next page was a photograph of five-year-old Nechama gazing into a lit candle. Nechama had never before noticed that her picture and Emunah's poem were back-to-back. The two women marveled at how their lives intertwined at so many pivotal moments.

Emunah agreed to speak at the Bat Mitzvah Club Banquet, knowing that she would tell this very story of her growing involvement in Judaism, her search for a meaningful way for her daughter to celebrate her Bat Mitzvah, and how Nechama Laber and the Rebbe's Candle Lighting Campaign had brought things full-circle.

Eliana celebrated a meaningful Bat Mitzvah after preparing with Nechama, but not at Disney World. Nechama Dina likes to share this story of Divine providence and how every good action we do can have a ripple effect that has an impact not only on our own family but throughout the world, as well.

It is truly amazing that after all these years, with all the original books having sold out and never having been reprinted, inspiring stories are still evolving from the original contest!

Thank G-d, the Bat Mitzvah Club has evolved and expanded over the years from Bat Mitzvah Camp to Jewish Girls Retreat, and in September 2014 it expanded to become Jewish Girls Unite, which is having a global impact on Jewish girls today.

THE BLESSING STANDS THE TEST OF TIME

by Peshe Razel Lieberman

The following story shows the Rebbe's current involvement in the Candle Lighting Campaign and this third Candle Lighting Writing Contest and book.

On December 8, 1976, I wrote to the Rebbe about my idea for a composition contest — with prizes — about lighting Shabbos candles. The purpose of the contest would be to encourage girls who don't yet light, and to help those who do light to become more involved.

After receiving my letter, the Rebbe called Mrs. Esther Sternberg, director of the Candle Lighting Campaign, and asked her to put my idea into action, and she and her staff carried the project to fruition. Although I initially suggested printing the winning entries in various publications, ultimately it was decided to publish a book entitled *A Candle of my Own*. Afterwards, the Rebbe sent me a letter saying: "I was pleased to receive your letter post-dated March 15th. It is gratifying to note that the composition contest has proved a great success, and may G-d grant you *hatzlocho* also in all other matters."

On Sept. 29, 2014, I wrote a letter to Mrs. Sternberg with my idea to help reignite enthusiasm for the Candle Lighting Campaign. The idea was to renew the composition contest (with prizes) on the internet, to continue it on an ongoing basis, and to publish winning entries right away online.

I could not find computer-savvy individuals who were able and willing to commit themselves to the project. To Mrs. Sternberg's great credit, she put in much effort to find the right people, and she even approached schools in her search for qualified women volunteers. Then, amazingly, I read on a Chabad news website, collive.com, about a *shlucha* in Troy, NY named Nechama Laber and her organization called Jewish Girls Unite, an online community for girls with a website, blogs, and an online candle lighting writing contest!

I emailed Nechama and attached a copy of the precious, validating letter the Rebbe had sent to me.

INTRODUCTION 15

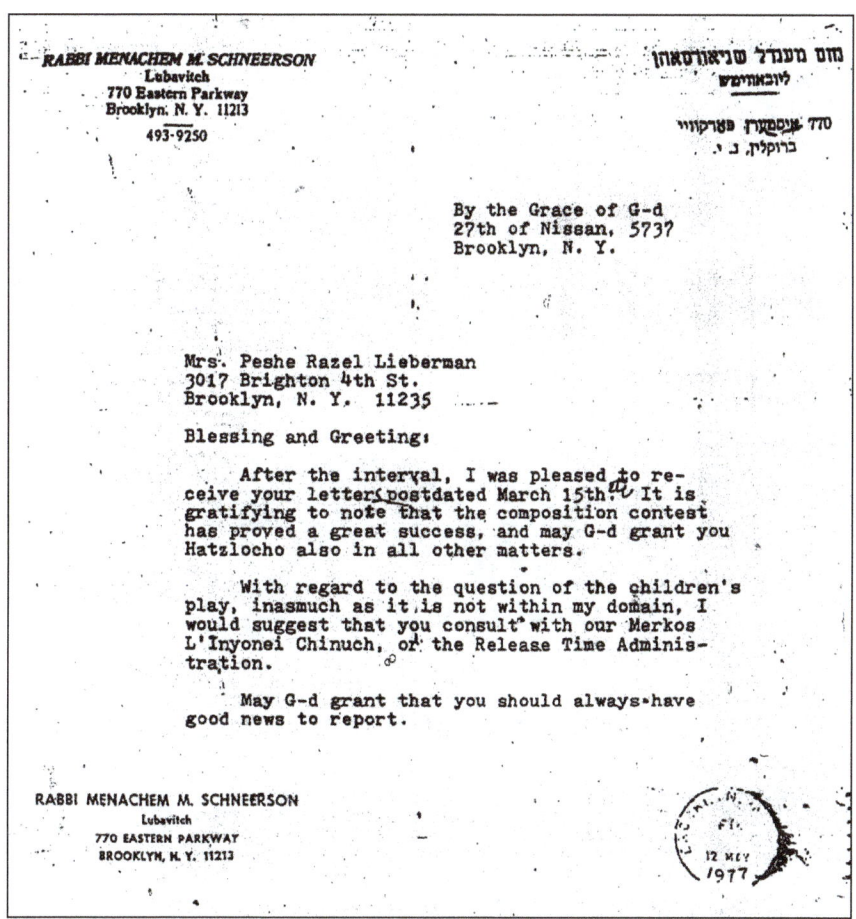

Nechama Laber called me on the phone, ecstatic with joy. She said that the date, March 15, mentioned in the letter is tremendously significant since March 15, 2015 was the exact date that Jewish Girls Unite was launched in Irvine, California, sponsored in honor of Meirah Schwartz's Bat Mitzvah by her parents Linda and Ory!

Nechama said, "While reading the Rebbe's letter to you, I felt as though the Rebbe was talking to me, too! We are already planning our First Anniversary Celebration on March 15, 2016, honoring Esther Sternberg!" (JGU certainly did so, very successfully.)

The JGU Global Celebration, with over 160 attendees at the Jewish Children's Museum and 800 viewers online, launched round two of the Candle Lighting Writing Contest with a goal to publish the third candle lighting book.

This story reflects great Divine providence and is just one more proof of the way the Rebbe's blessing, vision and advice are constant and continue to guide and inspire us.

JGU is a united, safe, online global community...

A community where girls feel loved and accepted by peers and mentors...

A safe online forum and blogs where girls share ideas, thoughts and feelings...

A variety of online programs and contests where girls connect through creativity and self-expression...

A place where girls meet, laugh, learn and share together in person at retreats...

A place where every girl can truly shine her inner light...

WELCOME TO JEWISH GIRLS UNITE!

www.JewishGirlsUnite.com

VISION STATEMENT:

We see all Jewish girls in the world connected online in a safe, loving, happy Jewish place at Jewish Girls Unite.

MISSION STATEMENT:

Our mission is to create a global community of empowered Jewish leaders and mothers, using innovative approaches in education, technology, and leadership development.

In our modern age, on so many levels the world is becoming smaller and experiencing more solidarity than ever before in history. The Rebbe would strongly encourage the use of modern communication methods to unite mankind. Long before the advent of the Internet, the Rebbe spoke about the power of technology to broadcast the Rebbe's own *farbrengens* via cable and satellite.

Simon Jacobson, in his bestselling book *Toward a Meaningful Life*, writes: "The Rebbe explains how people across the world, normally divided by space and time, are suddenly unified. It creates an opportunity for them to study together, pray together and resolve to do good deeds, causing a universal wave of togetherness. One might think, 'What can I possibly accomplish, sitting in one corner of the world made up of billions of people?' The Rebbe answers, **'Today we see how one person lighting a candle in one corner of the world can illuminate the entire world!'"**

JGU is a living example of how Internet technology is inspiring girls to joyfully unite in the goal of literally lighting up every corner of the globe!

♪ SONG
JGU "ONE MORE LIGHT" THEME SONG

This song launched the JGU One More Light Campaign on March 15, 2016.

Written and composed by Rivka Leah Cylich
Commissioned for JGU by Miriam Yerushalmi

Dedicated to every girl and woman and each one's ONE MORE LIGHT.

Did you hear the story told
As each soul comes to this world
It answers the purpose of creation

Do you believe that it could be
A single soul, like you or me
Could change the world and all we see forever

Plant a seed and watch it grow
Drop a stone, the ripples flow
Farther than you'd ever know

The sea is vast, the ocean's wide
But greater is your will inside
A simple act can change the tide

Yes I believe, like the sunrise each day
You light up the world each time that you pray

I believe like a flame burning bright
You shine through the darkness with each Friday light
A moment the world is waiting for
For you and your one more

Your one more light
Your one more light
Your one more light
Your one more light

Reach within to find your art
The colors that define your heart
Each of us can paint our part

Inspire me, I'll inspire you
You'll hit a wall, I'll pull you through
Heart and soul in everything we do

A million beats of a million hearts
Flames collide and outshine the stars
One melody with a thousand parts

Yes I believe, like the sunrise each day
You light up the world each time that you pray
I believe, like a flame burning bright
You shine through the darkness with each Friday light
A moment the world is waiting for
Let us light just one more

*Sheker hachen vehevel hayofi,
Isha yirat Hashem he tit'halal
T'nu la mipri yadeha,
Vi'yhaleluha bashearim maseha*

[Charm is deceptive and beauty is naught
A G-d-fearing woman is the one to be praised
Give her praise for her accomplishments
And let her deeds laud her at the gates*]

Yes I believe, like the sunrise each day
You light up the world each time that you pray
I believe, like a flame burning bright
You shine through the darkness with each Friday light
A moment the world is waiting for
Let us light just one more

Just one more light
Just one more light
Just one more light
Just one more light

I believe, like the sunrise each day
We'll light up the world

*Aishes Chayil - Psalms 91:11

Many of the songs in this book can be listened to at www.JewishGirlsUnite.com/songs.

Complete the Circle

Each Friday night, in every time zone around the world, women and girls bring in Shabbos by lighting Shabbos candles. As the Earth turns, New Zealand first welcomes Shabbos and begins the candle lighting circle. Afterwards people are busy greeting the Shabbos in Australia, yet it will not be Shabbos in Israel for another eight hours. Seven hours after that, New York girls and women light their candles and welcome in the Shabbos, and eventually California does the same. Alaska is the very last place on earth to usher in the Shabbos.

When you light your candles, know that you are in unity with millions of other Jewish women and girls in every time zone, around the globe, across Jewish divides and even generations — together participating in an age-old mitzvah.

You are part of this powerful candle lighting circle when you light your Shabbos candle with a blessing and prayer for peace for the entire world. The circle is not complete without you!

Your One More Prayer... Your One More Blessing... Your One More Light... Completes the Candle Lighting Circle!

Artist: Esther Ita Perez

You're invited to join the Candle Lighting Circle

WHO?
All Jewish women and girls from three years of age

WHAT?
Light Shabbos candles

WHEN?
Every Friday, 18 minutes before sunset

WHERE?
In the room where Shabbos dinner will be served.

HOW?
1) Give charity beforehand
2) Young daughters light one candle first with mother's help
3) Mother lights two candles
4) Spread and circle hands three times inward to welcome the Shabbos
5) Cover eyes with both hands
6) Recite the blessing below
7) Pray for all that you wish
8) Open your eyes and gaze at the candles
9) Wish "Good Shabbos" to family and friends

Shabbos Candle Lighting Blessing:

בָּרוּךְ אַתָּה אֲדֹנָ־י אֱ‑לֹהֵינוּ מֶלֶךְ הָעוֹלָם אֲשֶׁר קִדְּשָׁנוּ בְּמִצְוֹתָיו וְצִוָּנוּ לְהַדְלִיק נֵר שֶׁל שַׁבָּת קֹדֶשׁ.

Baruch A-tah A-do-nai, Eh-lo-hay-nu Meh-lech Ha-olam,

Asher Ki'-de-sha-nu B'-mitz-vo-sov, V' tzi-vanu L'-had-lik Ner Shel Shabbos Kodesh.

Blessed are You, Lord our G-d, King of the Universe, who has sanctified us with His commandments, and commanded us to kindle the light of the holy Shabbos.

See the appendix for blessings for other holidays.

ADDITIONAL PRAYER:

May it be Your will Lord, my G-d and G-d of my forefathers, that You show favor to me (my husband, my sons, my daughters, my father, my mother) and all of my relatives; and that You grant us and all Israel a good long life; that You remember us with beneficent memory and blessing; that You consider us with a consideration of salvation and compassion; that You bless us with great blessings; that You make our households complete; that You cause Your Presence to dwell among us.

Privilege me to raise children and grandchildren who are wise and understanding, who will love Hashem and fear G-d, people of truth, holy offspring attached to G-d, who will illuminate the world with Torah and good deeds and with every labor in the service of the Creator.

Please, hear my supplication at this time, in the merit of Sarah, Rebecca, Rachel and Leah, our Mothers, and cause our light to illuminate that it be not extinguished forever, and let Your countenance shine so that we are saved. Amen.

יהי רצון מלפניך ה' א‑לֹהינו וא‑לֹהי אבותינו שתחונן אותי (ואת אישי ואת בני ואת אבי ואת אמי) ואת כל קרובי ותתן לנו ולכל ישראל חיים טובים וארוכים, ותזכרנו בזכרון טובה וברכה, ותפקדנו בפקודת ישועה ורחמים, ותברכנו ברכות גדולות, ותשלים בתינו ותשכן שכינתך בינינו. וזכנו לגדל בנים חכמים ונבונים, אוהבי ה', יראי א‑להים, אנשי אמת, זרע קודש בה', דבקים ומאירים את העולם בתורה, ובמעשים טובים ובכל מלאכת עבודת הבורא. אנא שמע את תחינתי בעת הזאת, בזכות שרה ורבקה ורחל ולאה אמותינו. והאר נרנו שלא יכבה לעולם ועד והאר פניך ונושעה. אמן.

SHABBOS CANDLE LIGHTING GUIDE

Who lights the candles?

The woman lights and girls from the age of three (or younger, if the child can say the blessing).

The man lights if he is living alone or with no daughter over the age of 12. (If he has a daughter of 12 or older, she can light on his behalf.)

Why are women entrusted with lighting Shabbos candles?

Women are entrusted with this mitzvah because of their precious worth. This is a badge of honor for women indicating that *Hashem* has chosen them for these special roles.

A woman has the power to:

1. Give birth and raise children who will study Torah (Torah is light) and illuminate the world.

2. Increase and intensify peace and happiness on earth, starting with the tranquility and serenity (*Shalom Bayis*) at home resulting from the Shabbos lights.

3. Give her family length of days. Through this mitzvah, she earns the blessing of long life filled with goodness and vitality for her family. (*Zohar*)

Why do we light Shabbos candles?

1. *Shalom* - Peace in the Home: We illuminate our home so that we should not stumble in the darkness and create conflict.

2. *Oneg* - Pleasure: One must be able to see the food to fully enjoy the Shabbos meal.

3. *Kavod* - Honor the Queen: We add light in the home to welcome the Shabbos Queen.

What do the candles symbolize?

Shabbos is the day that brings illumination to our world, which often appears to be dark and negative. The candles represent the light of:

1. Torah and *mitzvot*

2. Our G-dly soul

3. The light of the "additional Shabbos soul"

Shabbos is a time to reconnect to our inner light. We can 'turn on the light' by learning Torah and fulfilling G-d's commandments, which transcend the darkness of the world and celebrate the light in our lives.

How do we prepare for Shabbos candle lighting?

The candles prepared should be sufficiently large (or the oil bountiful enough) so that the flame will burn for the duration of the meal.

The whole family prepares by putting on their special Shabbos clothes.

We give charity before lighting because when we give to others our own prayers are answered.

A daughter lights first so her mother can assist her with striking the match.

Where are the candles lit?

The candles should be lit in the room where the family eats to show that they are lit to honor Shabbos, and so that

everyone can enjoy the beautiful light of the Shabbos candles.

How many candles should be kindled?

Unmarried girl – Light one candle.

Married woman – Light two candles in honor of the two expressions G-d says in the Ten Commandments:

Shamor – We keep the Shabbos.

Zachor – We remember the Shabbos.

Some families' custom is that the woman of the house lights an additional candle for each child.

What time do we light?

The Shabbos candles are lit 18 minutes before sunset on Friday evening. You can check for the proper lighting time in your area at www.chabad.org.

Why don't we recite the blessing before we light the candles?

Although we ordinarily recite a blessing before we fulfill a mitzvah, when lighting Shabbos candles we light the candles first and then recite the blessing. This is because as soon as the blessing has been recited, the woman has accepted the Shabbos, after which it is forbidden to kindle a flame. Therefore, the custom is to light the candles, and then spread the hands inward in a circular motion three times to welcome the Shabbos.

Why do we cover our eyes when we light?

After lighting the candles, the eyes are covered in order to block the light while saying the blessing. Afterwards, when the woman or girl opens her eyes and looks at the candles to appreciate the light, it is considered as if she had recited the blessing before she lit the candle(s).

Once a woman recites the blessing, she has ushered in the Shabbos and the candles may not be extinguished or moved until the conclusion of Shabbos.

After the blessing is said, the gates of heaven are wide open to our prayers. Now, while your eyes are still covered, is an auspicious time to pray for your heart's desires.

♥ TIME TO REFLECT
CONNECTING TO THE TRUE YOU

Close your eyes gently.
Take a deep breath in.
Breathe out slowly.
Take another breath in, count 1,2,3.
Breathe out slowly, count 1,2,3,4.

Stretch slowly by moving your head from side to side. Relax your neck and shoulders.

Shabbos is here. Savor the warmth, the colors and beauty of the Shabbos atmosphere. You feel safe and calm. You are at ease. Shabbos was made just for you. It is a time to unwind, to connect to the true you.

Gaze at your Shabbos light and see the light of your own soul. See the light of your additional Shabbos soul. It is a gift from the One above. Shabbos uplifts you beyond all the challenges and chaos of the past week.

See the candle's flame soar higher and higher. On Shabbos, you ascend higher than you had ever dreamed possible, free to connect to *Hashem* as you were meant to, free to love your true self, free to genuinely love others.

Recall that *Hashem*, your source of life, has always been and will always be at your side. You have absolute trust that everything that was and will be is for the good of your soul.

Cover your eyes with your right hand and say: Hear, O Israel, the L-rd is our G-d, the L-rd is One. *Shema Yisroel Hashem Elokeinu Hashem Echod.*

I am the L-rd your G-d who brought you out of the land of Egypt to be your G-d; I, the L-rd, am your G-d. True.
You feel light and free. You feel inner peace and calm.

You are one with Hashem!

This is *Emet* — the true you!

Photo credit: Brenna Percy

CHAPTER 1:
Invite to Light

In this chapter, you will learn the power of inviting another Jewish woman or girl to participate in lighting candles. Do you realize how profound it is simply to invite someone else to join you in doing something? Many people are just waiting to be invited! Be the one to invite them to light Shabbos candles! Offer this book as a resource for their learning and inspiration... together we will be ambassadors of light.

STORY

THE POWER OF ONE MORE LIGHT

In 2001, there was a woman who studied in university, pursued her dreams, worked and traveled, and even lived in Israel for a year.

How could it be that she felt lost and empty?

One day she found a flyer at Rabbi Lazar and Rochel Lazaroff's Chabad House in Houston, Texas advertising a women's *Shabbaton* hosted by the Jewish community of San Diego at a hotel.

It was a life-changing weekend. She learned about the Candle Lighting *Neshek* Campaign.

She learned from Rabbi Manis Friedman that from the time of our first Matriarch Sarah 3000 years ago, women have been lighting Shabbos candles with their daughters. She discovered that Sarah's candles stayed lit all week, and that our Shabbos candles could also illuminate our homes and the world all week. She was very moved by these lessons, and she began to light Shabbos candles 18 minutes before sunset on a regular basis. She continued to grow in her Judaism through classes with her teacher, Rochel Lazaroff, and often spent Shabbos at their home.

She prayed to find a Jewish husband and wrote a letter to the Lubavitcher Rebbe asking for a blessing to establish a Jewish home built on the foundation of Torah and *mitzvot*. Two years later, she married a Jewish man named Ory, which means "My Light."

The above story is about Linda Schwartz.

> *How could it be that she felt lost and empty?*

Linda and her children today.

Meirah with her mother, Linda at the JGU Launch March 15, 2015 in honor of her Bat Mitzvah.

Today she is blessed with four children, including three daughters who light Shabbos candles with her each week.

Linda wanted to invite others to experience the same joy. Now, with Jewish Girls Unite, Linda has created the "Invite to Light Challenge" in honor of her daughter Sivan's Bat Mitzvah. Jewish girls and women can join the challenge at 1morelight.com.

"I'm delighted to personally invite others to be a part of the vital mission to reach every girl and woman to add one more light to the world."

Look at the power of One Candle:

One Shabbos candle... One more light lit by Linda so many years ago is spreading light to Jewish girls around the world today.

You, too, can be that candle! We invite you to share the light of Shabbos with your family and friends!

Linda Schwartz *is a member the JGU Global Leadership Team, the Founding Benefactor of Jewish Girls Unite and One More Light and the Underwriting Sponsor of the 1st JGU Creative Online Clubs.*

Dear Sivan,

I had to take a deep breath when I found this picture of myself as a little girl lighting Shabbos candles.

With what seemed like a flash and fast forward, I am now weeks away from celebrating the very special Bas Mitzvah of my second-oldest daughter — *you!*

I think about the journey my life has taken since that picture was taken and feel immense gratitude for even the twists and turns.

Looking back is always much easier than looking forward.

Each moment and meeting, up and/or down, played a role in navigating me to where I am today.

I was blessed with parents and a family who nurtured and loved me, encouraged and supported me, and gave me an education and a sense of who I was and where I came from.

As is true in every person's life, the journey depends on two things: choice and fate.

I want to speak to you about the "choice" part, as we both know Hashem is driving your fate.

Choose your thoughts. They give life to your speech and give motion to your movement.

Trophies and diplomas eventually collect dust. It is the

people you help, hold, and inspire that really matter.

Do not be fearless, but do not let fear stop you. Fear has a way of stopping people from doing great things.

You cannot have a voice without the risk of criticism. You cannot succeed without the risk of failure.

Work hard and remember there is no elevator to success: just the long winding staircase, which you are very well-equipped to climb.

Carefully plant seeds and be patient while they grow. Nothing worthwhile happens quickly. Be steadfast and determined. Stay kind and accepting. Be the

Lighting candles in Kever Maarat Hamachpela in Hebron, Israel where our Matriarch Sarah was buried.

common denominator.

May you always be a proud Jewish woman and IY"H in the right time, a wife and mother.

May you value your uniqueness and your role as a woman in the world.

You should never feel that you need to put on a pantsuit to feel equal or march publicly to announce your feminism in order to feel validated.

Women were created to do the things men cannot do.

The Rebbe says, "Distinctions are to be celebrated and harmonized as complementary manifestations of G-d's infinite capacity. A human body needs a heart and a brain in order to function. Both work very differently but neither is more or less valuable than the other. And such are the man and woman."

Live with momentum.

Trust your inner self — listen to the voice of intuition that knows the light of truth.

Believe that unanswered prayers are actually blessings. And revel in the fact that our Torah is eternal and timeless.

And never forget: you have choices.

Choose wisely.

Each choice you make will take you somewhere. Make sure it is a place you want to go.

And pray, pray, pray. Pray for the safety of our people, for health and recovery for those in need, success and simcha for all, and for the coming of Mashiach speedily in our days.

May Hashem bless you with revealed good, now and always.

I love you dearly,

Mommy

SILVER PAGE

In Loving Memory of Seymour Fox

Seymour Fox was an extremely busy attorney, completely devoted to accomplishing a fair result for his many clients. But as he rushed back and forth between appointments and courthouses, he was never too busy to see and help a person in need. If he saw a man on the side of the road who seemed to be in need of help, he would stop and ask him if he was okay, offer him a little encouragement and a bit of money. If he saw a woman in need, he would ask his woman passenger to go speak with her and give her a bit of money. He would rescue — chase down — stray dogs, and have someone go build a fence for the dog's owner so the dog would not be in jeopardy of running in traffic, alone and frightened, again. If the family seemed to be struggling to feed the dog, he would have dog food delivered.

The world is full of people — you and me and maybe strangers, maybe someone you know — who are lonely, a little forgotten by their family, or without family. We all have something to offer. Maybe a kind word, an ear to listen, a phone call, or some home baked cookies, a pretty card, a candle. We all can shine a light for ourselves, and someone else, to see that he or she matters.

THE SEYMOUR FOX FOUNDATION
IS PROUD TO SUPPORT OUR JEWISH DAUGHTERS!

In honor of Neshama Raquel Sari

We are so extremely proud of how you have become an ambassador of Jewish Girls Unite and "One More Light." You are a true Shlucha and role model for Jewish Girls of Creative Online Clubs, Bat Mitzvah and Beyond classes at JGU, and to all whom you meet anywhere you go. We are especially proud you are our daughter.

Your passion to encourage other Jewish girls and women to shine their holy light too is so powerful. We encourage you to always be the true Eishet Chayil that you are and always speak the truth in teaching the wisdom of our Jewish mothers Sarah, Rivka, Rachel and Leah through the lights of Shabbos and Torah and Mitzvos.

Always be humble in all that you do and accomplish. Never stop dancing your passion and beauty through music and art. Never stop expressing our beloved Rebbe's vision to empower all Jewish daughters. Never ever stop being loud and proud about shining your inner light from your neshama. Never stop using your gifts in writing.

"Zchor y'mos olam, binu shnos dor v'dor" - "Remember the days of old, reflect the generations of the past" to find your future. Never forget the generations of Jewish women who came before you. Neshama'le, remember always keep your candle burning and shining bright, Mazel Tov!

LOVE, EMAH AND ABBA

Age 3 Lighting Shabbos Candles Celebration
5767 / 2007

Continuing the traditions of our Jewish mothers Sarah, Rivka, Rachel and Leah.

Mazel Tov!
Bas Mitzvah
Nissan 27 - May 5
5776 / 2016

SONG
ARE YOU JEWISH?

Written by Leah Namdar at age 15 in England on a red bus, on the way back from weekly Mivtzoyim* to give out Shabbos candles.

To The Tune Of: Alone As A Camper

The heavens cried, the rain poured down
Hardly a soul on the streets to be found
But there in the distance a figure drew near
And as we approached her eyes filled with fear

"Are you Jewish?" She nodded her head
"My mother kept Shabbos, but not I," she said
"I've lived through Auschwitz, an orphan bereft,
Why should I do *mitzvos*? I have nothing left"

Chorus:
A mitzvah so precious, creating a bond strong and true
Between G-d in heaven and every Jew

I pressed a candlestick in her trembling hand,
"Please light it for Shabbos; you will understand"
With tears in her eyes, she accepted with grace
A smile lit up her wrinkled old face

Chorus

She kindled the flames on that Friday night
And whispered the *bracha*, her heart filled with light
The face of her mother smiled through the flames
"You've brought back the Shabbos to our home again"

Chorus

Many of the songs in this book can be listened to at www.JewishGirlsUnite.com/songs.

SHARING THE MITZVAH OF SHABBOS CANDLES

🗨 GLOBAL VOICES

SHABBOS CANDLES

When darkness falls on Friday night,
Jewish women and girls spread the light.
We set up the candlesticks copper, silver, gold,
And we do what our ancestors were told.
We wave our hands three times in the air,
And we rest them on our eyes in this holy atmosphere.
Shabbos is our only focus right now.
If you don't know the way to welcome Shabbos, I'll show you how.

Hannah Topol, Age 12
Beis Rebbe
California, USA

COME LET'S LIGHT

Come let's light,
An amazing candle light.
Nicely but carefully light it now,
so that Shabbos can come in.
Delicately light the beautiful Shabbos candle to greet Shabbos in a special way.
Love this mitzvah for it is done,
Every single Friday.

Let's light the Shabbos candles together NOW.
Invite the Shabbos Queen.
Get ready for Shabbos, she's on her way.
Have a Great Shabbos with your
Table glowing with Shabbos candles.

Batsheva New, Age 9
Hebrew Academy Community School of Margate
Florida, USA

INVITE TO LIGHT

I was trying to give Shabbos candles out but I couldn't find anyone to give them to. I finally found a lady and I asked her if she was Jewish. She said, "Yes, I'm Jewish." Then I asked her if she lights Shabbos candles. "No, I don't," she told me. So I offered her a candlestick and asked her if she wanted to start lighting Shabbos candles. The lady said, "YES!" It made me so happy to give out that special candlestick!

Chaya Furst, Age 9
Homeschool
New York, USA

I AM JEWISH

The house is small
Only two rooms
Lumpy bed
Wooden table
A single chair
A blanket of blackness

But then she comes
Dressed in white
Headscarf covering her hair
A regal queen

A matchstick in her hand
Strikes against the coal
Touches the waiting wick
A flame jumps forward
Reaching upwards
And suddenly

The room is an aura of bright light
Full of sparkling jewels
Shining pearls
The air is changed
Holiness charged

Her hands wave over the flames
One two and three
Covers her eyes

She prays
Sways
Beseeching to her Creator
A private time

Tears streaming from her eyes
Traveling down her face
Asking her Father
For help, support, everything she needs
And wants

It is years later
In Manhattan, New York
A young woman living in a big apartment

With large spacious rooms
A luxury bed
A cherrywood table
Many elegant armchairs
Epitome of richness

She is full
She is happy
Or so she thinks

But every Friday night
No candles are lit
The darkness is still there
Waiting to be extinguished

By those flickering orange lights

Her grandmother on high
Looks down, prays
Hopes with all her heart
That one day soon
She will strike that match

And light those candles
Just like her grandmother did
All those years ago

Friday afternoon
Rushing down the street
In all the crush of humanity

A young girl stops her
Eyes wide and innocent
She is holding two tea lights

Excuse me are you Jewish?
She asks
The young woman is shocked
Reminded of her past
Her heritage
Tries to find her voice
But no sound emerges

Yes, yes I am

She says loud and clear
I am Jewish
The girl hands her the candles
Tells her with a smile
Light these every Friday night
Help bring more light
Into the world

Friday night she stands
Eighteen minutes before sunset
Sets up her tea lights
On her cherrywood table

A matchstick in her hand
Strikes against the coal
Touches the waiting wick
A flame jumps forward
Reaching upwards

And suddenly
The room is an aura of bright light
Full of sparkling jewels
Shining pearls
The air is changed
Holiness charged

Her hands wave over the flames
One two and three
Covers her eyes
She prays
Sways

Beseeching to her Creator
A private time

Tears streaming from her eyes
Traveling down her face
Asking her Father
For help, support, everything she needs
And wants

And her grandmother on high
Looks down at her
And smiles

Rochel Danow, Age 16
Lubavitcher Girls School
Illinois, USA

SIDEWALKS OF TROY

I was walking on the sidewalks of Troy, New York, looking at the beautiful stores, holding the candle to give out. When I saw a woman, I asked her, "Are you Jewish?" She said, "Yes." I asked her if she lit candles. "I love it." she said. I gave her the candle, feeling so great!

Rivka Feldman, Age 10
New England Hebrew Academy
Massachusetts, USA

CONTINUE THE CHAIN

On Shabbos we can help someone else light
We can connect them to us that very night
Then they can connect to someone else
And together we can continue the chain
Which will bring *Moshiach* today.

Mushka Newman, Age 11
Bais Rebbe
California, USA

ACROSTIC SHABBOS POEM

Connect with *Hashem*
Amazing time
Nice clothing
Davening for the sick
Lighting before the sun sets
Excited for candle lighting
Let my sister hold my hand
It's special for me
Girls light candles, not boys
Have people make *brachos*
Together all girls light
Inviting guests to light also
Need candles and matches
Good Shabbos!

Chanie Geisinsky, Age 8
Cheder Chabad Girls of Long Island
New York, USA

SHABBOS WITH A FRIEND

Once there was a girl named Chana, who had a good friend named Sara. One day Sara invited Chana over for Shabbos, Chana didn't know anything about Shabbos but she still came. When Chana got to Sara's house she saw two candles and Sara said that it was time to light the candles. Sara showed Chana where her candle was and gave her a match and *Siddur*. Chana held the match and *Siddur* but she just stood there confused. Sara was about to light her candle when she realized that Chana looked puzzled. She asked Chana what was wrong and she answered that she didn't know about lighting Shabbos candles — she didn't even know what Shabbos was.

Sara explained the importance of lighting Shabbos candles. She told her that keeping Shabbos is one of the Ten Commandments. She also told her that you light candles to remind yourself it is Shabbos. Sara assured Chana that she would teach her more about Shabbos. Sara taught Chana the blessing to say and helped her say it after they lit their candles together.

Since then, Sara has been inviting Chana for Shabbos and Chana has been inviting Sara for Shabbos. Oh, and don't worry! Sara kept her word and helped Chana learn about Shabbos.

Liya Zarrinnia, Age 10
Emek Hebrew Academy
California, USA

A MEETING IN A MALL

"Shabbat candles" — the words struck my mind.

I was just walking in the mall with my father when a man approached us. He asked if we were Jewish. My father said that we have Jewish relatives on his mother's side. The man responded by saying, "That means you're Jewish." He asked my father to put on tefillin and then he gave me a Shabbat candle kit. He explained that when Jewish girls turn three they start to light Shabbat candles, which helps bring more light into this world.

Believe it or not, my sister Anna was turning three the following Saturday. What a coincidence that this man stopped us this week, so we could know about Shabbat candles before my sister's third birthday. Right away I felt a special connection to the Jewish people, to Shabbat, and to the Shabbat candles.

We went home and told my mother about our wonderful experience and the time we spent meeting this Jewish man in the middle of the mall. As we were telling our story, my mother started turning white. She told us the last time she lit Shabbat candles was when she was only 10 years old. She said she only lit because of her Jewish grandmother. Once her grandmother died, she stopped practicing her Jewish religion.

Right away my mother took the candle kit out of my hand. She set it up in a prominent spot for lighting and read the instructions, to remind herself how to light Shabbat candles with the blessing.

We found the contact number of the man, who turned out to be a rabbi, and my mother called him to thank him. She told him how thankful she was that he had found her family's Jewish spark. The rabbi invited us for a Shabbat meal and we went. We had a wonderful time. We have been going to classes and becoming more involved with the Jewish community. Amazing how one mall trip can change your whole life!

From that Shabbat, I have never missed lighting Shabbat candles. I even got my own silver candlestick as a present from my parents. Anna got a rose gold candle stick for her birthday too.

I can't wait a whole week till Friday. I get my special time with G-d and I feel like my great-grandmother is by my side watching me with a huge smile. I can't wait till I get to meet her. We have become more religious and are inspiring others to light Shabbat candles as well.

We are very happy with our new lifestyle.

I can't wait till next week, Friday in Jerusalem with my Jewish family.

Riva Rochel Chazanow, Age 12
Yeshiva Shaarei Tzion, New Jersey, USA

A DOUBLE MITZVAH

I have always created candlesticks over the years but for the past three years, I have been selling them at my mother's art shows and events. It has always been my passion for Jewish women to light Shabbos candles to bring more light, peace and goodness into the world.

A week ago at a Chanukah Art/Book Fair at Jewish Community Center event, I decided to also carry the Rebbe's gold candlesticks to give out free to Jewish women to light 'One More Light.' I chose to be a 'One More Light Ambassador' and so I encouraged them to sign up at www.1morelight.com. I gave them my card and I took their contact information to follow up with them and share the lighting every Friday night. I will send them weekly reminders and Shabbat Shalom wishes.

I was able to give out six of the Rebbe's gold candlesticks, and I also sold all of the candlesticks that I made and I then gave the money to *tzedakah*. A double mitzvah.

Neshama Sari, Age 12

Homeschool

Oregon, USA

EXCUSE ME, ARE YOU JEWISH?

I hear crashing waves bubble up on the sand.
Tall palm trees swaying in the soft breeze
Make me turn my gaze to the row of big beach houses
Standing with a gap between them

My back turned to the ocean
I see a beautiful woman in a yellow dress pass by.
Hand in pocket, I reach for the Shabbat candles.
I ask the woman, "Excuse me, are you Jewish?"

"Wow!" exclaimed the woman, and then burst into tears.
"Yes I'm Jewish, I have my grandmother's marvelous silver Shabbat candlesticks.
I have never wanted to light them until today.
Thank you for igniting my Jewish flame," the woman in the yellow dress said before she left.

Estee Wolfe, Age 12

Bnos Menachem

New York, USA

FOR A WOUNDED SOLDIER

Before I start this story, I need to tell you two things. First, my mother dislikes dogs (so do I, but that isn't part of this story), and second, one of our neighbors doesn't like us (but that is another story).

So my story begins in 2014 when the war in Israel broke out — "Operation Protective Edge," on July 8th. After many Jewish soldiers were wounded, a group of mothers in my school got together and organised *neshek* packages. Each contained the *brachos*, information about lighting candles in general, two tea lights, and the name of a wounded Israeli soldier who needed a healing. Between the three of us, my two sisters and I brought home four of these *neshek* packages.

On Friday afternoon, as Shabbos was fast approaching and everyone was busy getting ready, my mother saw these packages and felt that if she didn't give them out to the neighbours who live on our street, no one would be lighting candles for the soldiers. So my mother went to two of our friendly neighbours, who she knew would not refuse her and who would give her an extra boost to go on to our other neighbours. The third lady my mother went to was very receptive and open to the idea and asked my mother about the *brachos* and what she should do, so my mother showed her.

And then, my mother was left with one more *neshek* package and our unfriendly neighbour. She had an internal debate about what she should do. "They don't like us, but someone needs to light Shabbos candles for this soldier, but they don't like us *and* they have a dog..."

Finally, my mother courageously walked up the steps of the house and rang the doorbell. She still had thoughts of quickly leaving, but she remained rooted in her spot. When the lady finally opened the door, she rolled her eyes upwards as if to say, "What do you want?" My mother explained that the package contained the name of a wounded Israeli soldier and asked if she would be willing to light the candles for his recovery. As they stood there, the dog came barking and running outside and leapt onto my mother. She stood there calmly and said hello to the dog.

Later, when my mother told me about her experience, she said, "And I wasn't even scared of the dog!" At this last comment, I replied, "Of course you were not afraid — when you are busy with the Rebbe's Candle Lighting Campaign, the Rebbe is with you!"

And that Shabbos, our candles shone with an extra special glow.

Faigy Amzalak, Age 13
Beth Rivkah Ladies College
Victoria, Australia

♀ TIME TO REFLECT
SHARE YOUR LIGHT

Rabbi Tzvi Freeman sums it up perfectly in his book called *Bringing Heaven Down to Earth*.

"For hundreds of years, perhaps since the beginning of Creation, a piece of the world has been waiting for your soul to purify and repair it.
And your soul, from the time it was first emanated and conceived, waited above to descend to this world and carry out that mission.
And your footsteps were guided to reach that place.
And you are there now."

To fulfill my soul's purpose, all I need to do is look around and simply ask:
What is needed of me?
What can I do for someone else?
What can I do for the Creator of my soul?
Who can I invite to light?

So let's shine and share our light today, with Shabbos candles, kindness, prayer, and by using our unique gifts from *Hashem*. Together, we are making more of a difference than we can ever imagine – our light will keep shining forever.

❔ QUESTIONS TO CONSIDER

How would you invite another woman or girl to light? What would you say?

Share your answers at www.JewishGirlsUnite.com.

Photo credit: Sarah Greenfield

CHAPTER 2:

A Time to Pray

In this chapter you will learn that lighting candles offers you a precious gift: a time to pause and pray. Did you know that you can create a meditative prayer space every week when you light your Shabbos candles behind your covered eyes?

STORY

CREATING MY OWN PRAYER SPACE

Though I have been personally lighting candles since I was 20, I really did not know that I could use the moment to create a deeply personal and private space to pray. I have learned this through my work with JGU.

Now, when I light Shabbat candles and recite the blessing, I offer silent prayers with my hands still covering my eyes.

In the moment after I say the blessing, when my face is still covered with my hands, I take a moment to feel my warm breath, to look for and feel the safety and security of my Jewish soul. In that moment, I know that my soul and G-d are one. I feel connected profoundly and infinitely in that space.

Then, I take a moment to pause and create a prayer of gratitude:

> A personal blessing for those I love,
>
> A personal prayer for peace, for Israel, for my country, for our world, and
>
> A prayer for my heart's desire...that I may continue to share calm with our Jewish daughters around the world.

I have learned that all of this can happen in a moment — it truly can. I can step up to my Shabbat candles in chaos, and turn away from them in calm if I commit and really want to. With JGU in my heart all the time, I know that I am in unity with thousands of other Jewish

In that moment, I know that my soul and G-d are one.

women and girls around the globe, across Jewish divides — even across the generations — together participating in an age-old mitzvah. Together as we light Shabbat candles, united as one, we offer our world peace.

Susan Axelrod *is the JGU Global Strategy Advisor and Leadership Coach, Fundraising Coach and Consultant, Professional Speaker and Personal Mentor. She is the proud mother of Rebecca and Sarah.*

Artwork by Deborah Friedson

SILVER PAGE

*Dedicated to my daughters, Rebecca and Sarah...
With more love in my heart than they can imagine. XXOOM*

On Finding My Jewish Soul

I didn't realize she was missing... until she found me.

She peeked in and around all the stuff and baggage of my mind. She dipped her toe in. She retreated.

She felt lonely.

She yearned.

She came to the window of my heart and peered in for a long time; watching silently, cautiously,

It's unfamiliar...it's dark, is it safe? Then she saw light.

For years, she yearned; then she grew.

Finally, she became conscious; aware that All is Well, and that G-d is here.

SUSAN LOWENTHAL AXELROD

IN LOVING MEMORY OF
Rebbetzin Derorah Gutnick A"H

WIFE OF RAV SHALOM BER GUTNICK SHLITA - AV BEIS DIN OF MELBOURNE, AUSTRALIA

נפטרה כ"ג אלול תשע"ה

She served faithfully alongside her husband as Rebbetzin of Caulfield Shul, Melbourne Australia for over 48 years, and she taught after school Hebrew classes at the Shul, as well.

In 1954, at the behest of the Lubavitcher Rebbe, she founded the N'shei Chabad Women's Organization and was its president for over 35 years.

She merited to receive detailed and encouraging letters, as well as many blessings from the Rebbe throughout her life. Her legacy continues to shine through her children, grandchildren and great-children who are ambassadors of light.

Devorah Gutnick *Devorah Lerner* *Devorah Shapiro*

CONGRATULATIONS ON THE WONDERFUL WORK.

MAY IT BRING US TO THE ULTIMATE LIGHT OF MOSHIACH!

Leah & Yitzchok Gniwisch

HONORING THE LIGHT OF OUR TWO MATRIARCHS:

Mrs. Guta Schapiro,
our dear grandmother, who grew up in Leningrad, Russia. After surviving the Holocaust, she moved to Paris and today resides in NY.
With courage, faith and determination, she lit her Shabbos candles and kept the flame of Judaism burning in Communist Russia. She is a beacon of light for her dear descendants, who are illuminating the world as Shluchim of the Rebbe.

Mrs. Fradel Mishulovin,
our dear mother, our regal Shabbos queen. You bless us every week. Your light shines through your children around the world: NY, Canada, France, Australia, Israel and Russia too, bringing peace and light to usher in Moshiach! We Love You!

FROM YOUR CHILDREN & GRANDCHILDREN ACROSS THE GLOBE

My Dear Daughter,
Karen A"H.

You left us much too soon, but you continue to make your presence known from Shamayim.

As illness ravaged your body, your inner strength, sense of humor, concern for others, and your bright light shone through.

In your merit, our friend lit Shabbos candles for the first time on the Shabbos following your passing because she knew then that you would be with her.

Eight years later our friend continues to light Shabbos and Yom Tov candles, knowing you are there with her.

XOXOX Mom

DEDICATED TO MY BEAUTIFUL AND BELOVED MOTHER

Leah Masha bas Sarah Toiba

My mother implanted the kernels of Judaism within us... Shabbos candles, Pesach, visiting the sick, honoring parents, giving tzedakah, welcoming guests, learning, community activism, and even Moshiach's coming! She lived her life with passion and zest and a sense of optimism and enthusiasm.

Although no longer physically here, she often guides me with mature wisdom and kindness. She has inspired me to create my own warm, caring, beautiful, Jewish home.

She is my link back through the generations to Sarah Imeinu and I will forever walk by the light and warmth and love of my mother's Shabbos lights.

TZIVIA CHAYA ROSENTHAL

Miriam Fellig, a Holocaust survivor, a strong woman who raised 10 children and devoted her life to them. She is honored to live among almost all of them and be surrounded by her grandchildren and great-grandchildren.

♪ SONG

I USED TO THINK MY MOTHER WAS THE SHABBOS QUEEN

Composed by Yocheved Reich
Sung by Chanale Fellig

I used to think my mother was the Shabbos Queen
She stands so regally with royal grace
And whispers to the King of the Universe, *Hashem*
From a very special place, behind her covered face

I know that she's not asking Him for diamonds
My noble mother doesn't ask for gold
She's asking Him to help me study all the Torah's ways
And to let her eyes behold the joy as she grows old

Chorus:
Oh, and when I grow up
No matter what life brings
Hashem will give me the strength I need to handle it
And I will walk by the lights
Of a thousand Friday nights
And the *tefillos* of my mother, who always had her candles lit

My mother turns our house into a palace
Her wisdom and her warmth both make it so
She *bentches licht* and I can hear her tender feelings speak
Without any voice or words but the kiss on my cheek

Chorus

Each mitzvah that I do will be a diamond
Each smile I give will be a precious stone
To put into the crown she seems to wear on Friday night
And when I am fully grown, I'll wear a crown of my own

Chorus

♪ SONG
MIRACLES GO ON

By Tzivia Kay

With Your help, I stay strong,
I dedicate another song,
to You my Lord, to You my Lord.
Every moment is a gift,
and every chance I get I lift
my eyes to Your throne,
but only You can see us all.

Chorus:
Every second miracles go on
You send them down, You send them down,
and if only people noticed
there would be mercy, peace and love,
all over this chaotic world

With Your help, I stay strong
as my soul sings this song
to You my Lord, to You my Lord
I am brave when You're here
You're beside me
I've felt You all along
I'm not alone

Chorus:
Every second miracles go on
You send them down, You send them down
and if only people noticed
there'd be mercy, peace and love
all over this chaotic world

You've given me all I have
You've helped me through each way
You are so good to me
and all I do, and all I do is pray

Chorus:
Every second miracles go on
You send them down, You send them down
and if only people noticed
there would be mercy, peace and love
all over this chaotic world

Many of the songs in this book can be listened to at www.JewishGirlsUnite.com/songs.

💬 GLOBAL VOICES

PERSONAL PRAYERS

SHABBAT LIGHT

I see her looking at the Shabbat light,
Even though it is very bright.
And I think to myself,
What are her thoughts this very night?
What might she be asking?
And what might she be praying?
It may be for health.
And it may be something more
But I ask myself,
What would I ask for?

Rachel Niyazov, Age 12
Yeshiva Sha'arei Zion
New York, USA

PRIVATE TIME WITH THE KING

Imagine you had a private audience with the king. What would you do?

Would you waste it?! Or would you spend your time wisely speaking to the King when he is closely listening?

Lighting candles is just the same. You are standing before the King. It's your time, when you light Shabbos candles, to tell *Hashem* whatever you want. This is your special opportunity. Candle lighting is a special time for women and girls to talk to *Hashem* privately and closely for as long as they want.

When I light candles, I think about the week behind me and see what I want for the next week to be better. I ask *Hashem* anything I want. I ask for *Moshiach* and think about anything that has bothered me over the past week and I ask Him to fix it.

It is a time when you are welcoming in the Shabbos Queen and your *neshama yeseira*, additional soul. What a wonderful opportunity!

Wishing all Jewish women and girls the strength to take advantage of this special time and beautiful mitzvah to its fullest.

Rivka Herszberg, Age 8
Beth Rivkah Primary
Melbourne, Australia

I ASK HASHEM

I strike the match and watch the flame ignite
The glow is soft, pretty and bright
I wave my hands over my eyes
And ask *Hashem* that I hear no cries
As I watch the beautiful flames flicker
Faster, lower, higher, quicker
And so I ask the One Above
To bring back down those who we love
Anu Rotzim Moshiach Achshav!

Chera New, Age 12
*Hebrew Academy Community
School of Margate
Florida, USA*

I LOVE TO WATCH THE FLAMES

On Friday, before sunset I love to look out the window and wait to watch the beautiful sunset, until it's time to light Shabbos candles. When I strike the match I love to watch the beautiful flames burst onto the match, then watch the flames calm down.

As I light my candlestick I enjoy watching the wick burn into a gorgeous flame. Then I wave my hands three times over the fire and cover my eyes to say the prayer. When I say the prayer it's like I'm in a different world: a world of peace, quiet, and calmness.

I have the opportunity to ask G-d, our King, for anything and pray for anyone for as long as I wish to because G-d is waiting for me to pray and He's listening to me.

As I uncover my eyes, I love to hug my mother and wish everyone Good Shabbos. Then I just sit on the couch and read a book and watch the gorgeous Shabbos candle flames dance around peacefully until my father comes home from *shul* to make *kiddush* and we eat the delicious Shabbos meal. I wish Shabbos and its peace could last forever!

Ita Gurevich, Age 12
*Bnos Menachem
New York, USA*

IT IS AN AUSPICIOUS TIME

When the sun goes down, all girls and women, starting from the age of three, light Shabbos candles to welcome the Shabbos Queen. It is a very special mitzvah that girls and women have the privilege to do.

When we light candles, it is an *eis ratzon*, an auspicious time, so we ask *Hashem* for many good *brachos*, like a *refuah* for the sick, to do well on a difficult test, or to bring *Moshiach* now! Good Shabbos!

Vichna Edelkopf, Age 8
*Cheder Chabad Girls of Long Island
New York, USA*

SHABBOS CANDLES

When girls and women light Shabbos candles, it is a way to connect to *Hashem* and to ask for your needs and wants. Like a child asks her father.

Shabbos candles help keep peace in the home because if there were no candles in the olden days then people would trip over each other and pour soup down each other's backs. Now it is just a spiritual part of Shabbos. That is the holiness of Shabbos candle lighting.

Zoey Atias, Age 12
Bader Hillel Academy
Wisconsin, USA

I THANK HASHEM

Every Friday night
The candles that we light,
They make the whole world so bright.
In front of the candles I stand,
My eyes covered by my hands.
I think about how my week was,
And I thank *Hashem* for all that He does.
It's a time to ask for anything,
For we are standing right in front of the King.

Sara Gerber, Age 9
Cheder Chabad of Philadelphia
Pennsylvania, USA

LIGHTING TOGETHER

As she looked at the blazing yellow light in front of her, she *davened* for her family and self. A rich feeling overcame her: a feeling of joy and achievement. As she looked up to the heavens she thanked *Hashem* for the present of the Torah and the ability to light the Shabbos candles.

Now at this very moment, she joined with millions of women and girls around the world uniting as one and welcoming the Shabbos Queen. She cried out to *Hashem* for a *Refuah Shelaimah* for *Klal Yisroel*, thinking of those less fortunate than she, those who can't physically light candles tonight. She prayed that by next Shabbos we could all light Shabbos candles together in *Yerushalayim* with the *Beis Hamikdash*!

Chaya Blackman, Age 13
Beth Rivka School
New York, USA

I HEAR MY BREATH

When I light Shabbos candles
I am still
I hear my breath
And I feel my *neshama* connected to *Hashem*.
I bring in the light towards me
I say the blessing with my
eyes behind my hands
I am still
I hear my breath
And I feel my *neshama*
connected to *Hashem*.
I ask *Hashem*, not only
for myself but for others
I am still
I hear my breath
And I feel my *neshama* connected
to *Hashem*.
With the New Year coming
I wish you all
A year of health and happiness.
May we all see peace for Israel and the
Jewish nation.
May we find time every day
To be still
Hear our breath
And feel our *neshamot* connected to
Hashem.

Lielle Schwartz, Age 10
Long Beach Hebrew Academy
California, USA

FLAMES SO HOT

Flames so hot
Wax melting down
As I wave three times over the candles
I put my hands over my eyes and say

"Baruch atah Hashem,
   elokeinu melech haolam,
      asher kidishanu
         bemitzvotav vetzivanu
            lehadlik ner shel
               Shabbat kodesh."

I think of all the things
   that I need
And my faith in *Hashem*
I think of my family and friends,
And how life would be
If I never lit Shabbos candles
And if I didn't have the key

I think of this every Friday night
As I uncover my hands

Devorah Bracha Kessler, Age 12
Beis Rebbe School
California, USA

> *When I light Shabbos candles I am still I hear my breath*

Shabbat candles

I think lighting shabbat candles is special because it really feels like I'm really really close to Hashem and I feel it is a special oportunity to light the candles. I dont know what I'd do without shabbat candles. It is also a special time to ask Hashem to bless us. By Mimi Gerschman year two 5J

Mimi Gerschman, Age 8
Beth Rivkah Primary, Melbourne, Australia

YOU CAN ASK

There is a certain time each week,
That you will have a chance to speak.
That time is when you do light
The Shabbos candles Friday night.
Now listen folks, let me tell you,
There's lots of things for you to pray.
You can ask *Hashem* for food and health,
You can ask *Hashem* for success and wealth,
You can ask *Hashem* for babies too,
You can ask *Hashem* to guide you.
Don't forget to use this chance to pray
For *Moshiach* to come today!

Musia Simpson, Age 9
Shluchim Online School
Ohio, USA

I DAVEN TO HASHEM

As I light the Shabbos candles,
I *daven* to *Hashem*,
I say my many *tefilos*
With tears... rolling down my face.

Then... I think of those many families in *Eretz Yisroel*
Who are now broken forever...
By terrorists, killing innocent people they've never known.
A father?! A mother?! A teen?! A child?! A baby?!
What did THEY do to them?! Nothing!

We all *daven* for them and everyone to be safe,
We see in some stories, openly how our Father answers our *tefilos*.

As I uncover my eyes, the tears still gliding slowly down my face,
I watch my candle, my fire, burn and soar up high, as if sending the message to The One On High.

Comforted by that knowledge, the sparkling light of the candles and the holiness of Shabbos,
My tense body, face glowing now with radiance, miraculously calms down to a peaceful and restful feeling.

I watch my candle burning, and I see the message *Hashem* gifts me every single week.

I lower my hands slowly and turn to look at my mother, who stands there still, holding her whispered prayers in close to her fluttering eyelids. She *davens* passionately and desperately for every one of her children, and I ask *Hashem* for one last wish.

I ask that when my mother is ready to look back at the candles, she sees that every one of her children will be safe and sound this week again.

I hope she knows that with every wick she sparks for us, she rekindles our promise from *Hashem*. My mother and I, we light our candles, and because we do so, it is we who keep our family safe. Well, only because we always know that *Hashem* is not far behind us.

Shayna Ceitlin, Age 15
Beis Rivka Montreal
Montreal, Canada

⚐ TIME TO REFLECT
YOUR PRAYER

PAUSE:
- What is your mission? What do you wish to accomplish?
- Visualize the world as you would like it to be.
- What do you wish for yourself, your loved ones, your world?
- Why are you grateful?

PRAY:
- For inner peace and happiness to handle the challenges you may face.
- To *Hashem* for your physical needs to provide the means to accomplish your soul's mission.
- Express your thanks to *Hashem* for your warm home, your beloved family, your own light, the light of Shabbos, and the power to transform darkness into light.

BE PRESENT:
- After candle lighting uncover your eyes and gaze at the candles with fresh eyes. Bask in the beauty of the candles, as if for the first time.
- Acknowledge the passionate fire of your infinite soul.
- Savor the beauty of the light of each family member.
- Good Shabbos!

❓ QUESTIONS TO CONSIDER

What is your personal prayer to Hashem when you light? Who needs your prayers this week?

Share your answers at www.JewishGirlsUnite.com.

Photo credit: S. Roumani

CHAPTER 3:
Light Up Your Soul

In this chapter, you will learn how lighting Shabbos candles can help you find your Jewish soul-connection. Did you know that when you take a breath, in that moment your mind clears and you can find inner quiet? When you light your candles find that inner quiet and look for your soul's desire, your soul's direction. This is where you will find Hashem!

STORY

A CANDLE IGNITED MY SOUL

Many times people ask me, "What inspired you to become a *Baalas Teshuvah*, returnee to Jewish observance?" They continue, "What gave you the strength at such a young age to make such a commitment?" I never really knew. I myself was unsure. I would answer "Hmm, I just don't know." But recently after so long, the dots all connected.

I remember, at the young tender age of about seven, going to the Israeli March in Rancho Park, California. I was especially connected to Israel because I was born there, and I remember making the effort to be part of the Israeli March. Boy, was I ever happy when after walking for so long, I finally arrived at the Israeli Festival grounds. Seeing all the people together reaching our destination, I felt as if we were really landing in the Holy Land! Although I was a bit tired, I felt ever so exhilarated and thrilled to be part of my people! At the park, there were the smells of Israeli food, falafel, shawarma - but the excitement didn't stop there. There were so many different booths to inspire people to get closer to Judaism. I remember the first booth I stopped at — gazing at those shiny golden candlesticks, wanting to own one.

I dared not get too close to the man dressed in a black suit with a black hat because I didn't see how this could be mine. I didn't have money to buy such a high-priced commodity, and I was afraid I would just be so disappointed. As I was standing there, the man turned my way holding the shiny gold candlestick kit, and with a smile said, "This is for you." I thought…"For me, for free?" I was shocked and I thought for sure there must be a mistake. That's when I saw him giving out more kits to other girls. I kept thinking, "Wow, what a kind man!" as I happily took one.

I totally remember feeling so privileged to have received the golden candlestick and guarded it the whole day. The fair was over and the countdown began. I couldn't wait until Friday to finally be able to light it.

Every day was forever until that holy day came. The intense feelings which I felt that day finally bridged over to Shabbos itself, and I felt so serene and so connected to Israel and to my people.

Miraculously, I was invited to celebrate Shabbos fully at several observant people's homes and nurtured the spark that was ignited by the experience of lighting Shabbos candles. Mrs. Miriam Rabinowitz, my school teacher, invited me over and over again to her lovely Shabbos table. My very best friend's parents, Freida and Ephrayim Blum, opened their home to me on Shabbos and every day of the week, and they also brought me to the B'nai Akiva Shabbos programs. The joy and warmth at the Shabbos table solidified my love for Shabbos and for Judaism. Receiving the bright shiny Shabbos candle started it all!

Thank you, Lubavitcher Rebbe, for sending your *shluchim* to Rancho Park. Thank you, Rebbe, for caring that I as a little girl would have a chance to ignite my Jewish soul. ....So now I can say that it was the flame of these Shabbos lights which ignited the flame of my soul!

Miriam Yerushalmi *is a member of the JGU Global Leadership Team and the recipient of the 1st JGU Creative Educators Award. She is an author and lecturer. She practices marriage and family counseling using Chassidic teachings and Tanya.*

The candlestick that Miriam received was designed by the Lubavitcher Rebbe and can still be purchased for distribution at www.jewishgirlsunite.com.

> *"I remember the first booth I stopped at – gazing at those shiny golden candlesticks, wanting to own one."*

Letter to My Dearest Daughter, Chana Leah Yerushalmi

My Dearest One and Only Beloved Daughter,

We are always together forever; you are my light, you are a flame constantly shining bright.

I would like to give you this eternal gift so that when you light your Shabbos candles and gaze at the holy flame and usher in the holy peaceful Shabbos, you will recall the Chassidic teaching — "G-d is a devouring fire" — this is a message to us of how much he loves us.

In fact, Hashem is lovesick over us; knowing that will help us worship Hashem with Hitlahavus — fervor; burning passion, enthusiasm.

Through Hashem's Torah and mitzvos we can reach a level of total Deveikus — attachment to Hashem. So when we see the flame of Shabbos we think "Boiyi Kallah" — come my beloved Bride.

Kallah means not only the holy bride that comes to greet us, but Kallah also means "burning"; when Shabbos comes, all the mistakes and all the negativity of the past week burn away from the presence of the holy light.

When Shabbos enters, through our igniting the light, our burning, yearning heart is ready to experience a soul ascent.

Ready to capture the rapture of Oneness unfolding; unifying us all no matter where we are, near or far.

I pray as you see the holy flame you see the fire in you.

As you see the light, I pray you see the light within you.

You are my life.
You are a shining star forever.
Forever we are together.

LOVE, IMA (MIRIAM YERUSHALMI)

Artist: Esther Ita Perez from the book "Let's Go to Eretz Yisrael"

Goldy Rosenfeld

WE LOVE YOU AND
ARE SO PROUD OF YOU!

Love, Your Family

Brayden Arielle Gross

You are such an inspiration to us and to so many others. Just as you continue to light your Shabbos candle each Friday night, you also light up the world around you each and every day! We are so proud of you!

Love always,

Mommy, Daddy and Shyloh

Safta Sabina Ferber

Our Safta, Sabina Ferber, was a Holocaust survivor who came to America, opened a successful tailor shop, and made beautiful dresses and hats.

Every Shabbat at Kiddish at shul, she would sit at a table, and recount stories of her life in Poland, Russia, and Israel, with many avid listeners. Her stories were filled with details, and she had a good sense of humor, even though she had a really hard life.

She taught us an important lesson in life, that in order to survive hard-times you have to learn a useful trade.

Our Safta's legacy is that she taught us how to be strong, resourceful and independent women.

YAFFAH & SHOSHANA FERBER

TO SUSAN, NECHAMA
& RABBI LABER FOR
YOUR INSPIRATIONAL
EFFORTS ON BEHALF
OF JEWISH GIRLS
EVERYWHERE!

—ED & LAURA JACOBS

Passing the eternal flame from generation to generation.

Torah & Mitzvot, Love & Kindness

—RAIZEL, CHANA SIMCHA BAT OFRA YOSEFA FELD BAT RIVKA SHAINDEL LIEBOW

In honor of my deeply beloved mother, **Joyce Weinberg Newman** who, with no formal Jewish education, committed herself to igniting the Neshomas of all her children. Her devotion to tradition, education and Yiddishkeit is resulting in bright perpetual flames carried on within each of her many grandchildren.

All of her children and grandchildren are spiritual, Shomer Shabbos, devout Yidden. May our mother continue to go from strength to strength, while she spreads Torah and light over us all.

—VANESSA NEWMAN

IN LOVING
MEMORY
OF

Tata Rachel Bouskila

MAY OUR CHILDREN GROW
STRONG AND SHINE WITH
THE LIGHT OF TORAH.

—CLAUDIA ALLOUCHE

SONG

SHINE YOUR INNER LIGHT

*By Rivka Leah Cylich, commissioned by Linda Schwartz
for the launch of JGU on March 15, 2015.*

In those times
When you find
That each door that you try
Is locked, yet again, and it won't let you by,
In your heart lies the key
Look inside and you'll see
Believe
Just Believe

In those days
In the haze
When all you see is true
Seems to fall far behind
And you're lost within you
And you try to be strong
But it's hard to hold on
For so long

Chorus:
Trust your inner light
(clap clap)
Shadows fall away
(clap clap)
Hold your candle high
(clap clap)
Night will turn to day
(clap clap)

Moments when you're feeling small
No reason to give in
Don't you know in the greatest darkness
Light will always win

So be the miracle I believe in
Be the candle burning bright
You can be the flame we're reaching for
Light up, light up the night

Chorus

Don't you know, this place in time
Is waiting just for you
To learn, to give, to love, to live
There's so much you can do

So be the miracle we believe in
Be the candle burning bright
You can be the flame we're reaching for
Light up, light up the night

SO…
Shine your inner light
(clap clap)
Shadows fall away
(clap clap)
Hold your candle high
(clap clap)
Night will turn to day
(clap clap)

Many of the songs in this book can be listened to at www.JewishGirlsUnite.com/songs.

GLOBAL VOICES

SHABBOS CANDLES LIGHT UP OUR SOUL

THE CANDLE OF MY SOUL

I shut the door softly. But it was too late.

"Where are you going?" nine-year-old Abby asked. Do little sisters need to know everything?

"Just going to Jessica's," I said, quickly walking away from more questions.

My feet, by habit, started to turn right, but I quickly turned left towards the forest. I thought to myself, *Why should I go the long way and have time to ponder all my troubling thoughts? The shortcut is a bit prickly and uneven, but it will distract me and get me there more quickly.*

I began walking quickly. And I tried — I *really* tried — not to think about my life and how it had changed since Daddy died. It had been ten whole years. I was just five. Why think about it now? But I knew why. Now that I'd reached the age of fifteen, I felt that I want to know where my life was headed. Maybe that's why I chose Jessica, the life of the party, as my friend — to get away from my thoughts. But I could never run away from the future.

I tripped over a rock and it brought me back to reality. *Where am I?* I thought. *The place is not familiar and it doesn't look like Jessica's neighborhood. Uh oh! I'm lost. It's getting dark and I've even forgotten my phone.*

I looked around. There were a few small houses. I went to the one that looked the lightest and knocked on the door. A man with a short beard and a black hat and jacket answered. He said something but I didn't hear; I was focused on the captivating scene in front of me.

There ahead, I could see a lady and two girls with their eyes covered, standing in front of beautiful candlesticks with dancing flames. Suddenly a scene came to my mind. I was a girl of five with pigtails, ribbons, and a dress. I was standing next to a lady who seemed to be Mom but looked a bit different. Suddenly it hit me: Shabbos. Shabbos candles.

The mother and the girls by the candles finished and walked toward me, peering at my pale face.

"Are you okay? Please sit down. What is your name?" the mother asked me.

I sat down on the edge of a chair.

"I'm Orlee," I whispered hoarsely.

"Sh-sh-Shabbos. C-candles."

"You're Jewish!" the younger girl said.

"Well, we used to be. But after my father died, ten years ago, my mother — well, she didn't really want to be religious anymore." I explained.

"Orlee, you are a Jew, and forever you will be one," the mother told me.

The family did not seem to mind my miniskirt and short sleeves as they explained the gift of Shabbos to me. They invited me to stay for the meal, but I needed to digest everything that had just happened. They gave me directions and I walked home, completely forgetting Jessica.

When I came home, Mom was sprawled on the couch, reading. Abby was at her side, explaining how she could go to sleep late that night because it's the weekend and she knew how to sleep in like Orlee.

"Hello Orlee, glad you're home. How was Jessica's?" Mom asked me.

I kept quiet.

"Mom, w-why why can't we be Jewish? Why can't we keep Shabbos? Why can't we light Shabbos candles? I want to, Mom — I really want to light Shabbos candles. It's so special, so —"

"NO, NO AND NO! No way are you lighting Shabbos candles in my home! And don't you mention this again!" Mom yelled angrily and marched up to her room.

I noticed Abby in the corner of the room, shocked, weeping quietly. She had never, ever seen her calm mother like this. And she didn't know what this was all about. She barely knew what it means to be a Jew. One day she will, I promised myself, no matter what.

"Orlee, what did you do?!" she said, as if I had committed some kind of crime. She ran up to her room, too.

And then I, Orlee Segal, was all alone in the family room. But I felt like I was all alone in the world.

* * *

"Look at the sun starting to set. It's stunning!" Abby exclaimed, exactly a week later.

My stomach twisted. I bet there were more knots in there than in Abby's old, tangled jump rope, still somewhere in the back of her closet.

I knew what this meant. It was time to light Shabbos candles. And that's what I was about to do.

"Are you all right, Orlee? You look like a ghost!" Abby told me.

"One minute." I said to her, running into the privacy of my room. Too bad the lock was broken, but at least Mom had gone out shopping. Last week, after "it" happened, Mom acted as if nothing had happened.

I searched through my purse, vaguely remembering the day around a month or two ago when I went to the mall with Jessica.

"Excuse me, are you Jewish?" someone had asked me.

"Uh, yeah." I had mumbled.

"Would you like to light Shabbos candles?" she had asked.

"Oh, just come on, Orlee," an annoyed Jessica had said.

I had grabbed the outstretched Shabbos candle kit and stuffed it into the back of my bag. I had totally forgotten about the treasure in my purse until now.

"Ah! Here it is." Now I took the candle and set it out on my desk. I struck a small match and lit the candle. I read the blessing in English.

With tears in my eyes, I added my own prayer to G-d.

"G-d, I don't know why, but I really, really want to be Jewish. I want to light the candles, the Shabbos candles. I never felt this way before, but I wish Mom, Abby and I could be lighting these candles together."

At this point, I really was crying.

The door suddenly opened. My heart nearly stopped. Abby walked in and stopped short at the sight. The room smelled of strawberry shampoo. I didn't turn around. I was still awed by the magnificent candle being rained on by my tears.

I thought Abby would shriek but she just stood there, mouth hanging open. She seemed to also be awed by the candle.

Suddenly there was a voice. I froze. If you would try to count how many times my heart beat in that one minute, you would have to create a new number.

"Hi, girls. The store was closed so I just went to the accessory store nearby. I also —" My mother stopped mid-sentence as she entered the room, shocked.

> *I was still awed by the magnificent candle being rained on by my tears.*

I glanced behind me. There was open-mouthed, frozen Abby. And behind her was Mom, standing there frozen as well. Her face was so white, whiter than the stack of tissues on the floor, whiter than my freshly washed sheet — pure, pure white.

It looked like she wanted to say something so I waited and waited. And I waited. My heart slowed down to a normal pace and I even felt a feeling of calmness, serenity and tranquility. I waited a bit more until Mom spoke in the calmest, most pleasant of voices I have ever heard her speak in.

"Shabbat Shalom."

Sara L. Weisberg, Age 11
Bnos Yaakov
New Jersey, USA

SHABBOS AT JEWISH GIRLS RETREAT

I was running around camp, and it was an hour before Shabbos. Between finishing my jobs and getting ready for Shabbos, I was nervous but excited. In my secular life I didn't keep Shabbos fully but it was something I wanted to do in the future.

After showering I felt refreshed, and excited for Shabbos to begin. I put on my beautiful Shabbos dress, stockings, and shoes. Shabbos was a time I looked forward to, since it was peaceful and lovely. I walked out of my bunk house to the dining room. During the walk I reflected on the week — it was fun but a lot of hard work.

As I got up to the dining hall, where we lit Shabbos candles, I was ready for Shabbos to come. I saw my friend and coworker Mimi. "Hi Mimi, good almost-Shabbos."

"Good almost-Shabbos to you too, Sarah."

The campers were decorating candlesticks, chatting, and eating a snack since dinner would be quite late.

"Hello Sarah, how are you?" "Good, and you?" "Good." Usually I felt tired, but today I felt elated!

"Okay girls, now it's time to light Shabbos candles," the head counselor said. I went up to the candle and struck a match. As soon as the match was lit I was in my own little world. I lit the candle and said the blessing. Then I added my own blessing asking for my family to be safe and well. I went back into the beautiful reality that was Shabbos. I admired the candles, seeing how they danced and how they lit up the room. It was a Good Shabbos indeed.

Sarah Salles, Age 15
West Broward High School
Florida, USA

SPARK

Every woman is a special candle
Waiting to be lit
She just needs that small spark
To *Hashem* she can commit.

Against all wind and rain
It's hard to stay aflame
But when we all unite together
We will be unbreakable forever.

Each flame we must ignite
To push away the dark and windy night
There is always a blazing fire
Waiting to be admired.

Rivky Laskar, Age 13
Beis Rebbe
California, USA

I DREAMT OF CANDLES IN THE NIGHT

Brocha Jacobs, Age 10
King David Primary School
Birmingham, England

A CANDLE IN SOMEONE'S HEART

Light a candle in someone's heart.
Lighting a candle in a heart means lighting up someone's *neshama*.
You can do that by teaching them about Torah and *mitzvot*.
That will take us out of *golut* and will bring the *geulah*.

Leah Amzalak, Age 8
Beth Rivkah Primary
Melbourne, Australia

FOREVER

The match strikes
Erupting in flames
Slipping towards the wick
Licking its threads
Casting forth a glow
Forever

She passes the shaded window
Her heart skips a beat
The faint spark
The small flame
Has tugged her heart
Forever

But as she observes it flicker
She awakens
The spark that
For so long was silent
Bursts into flames
Forever

One Shabbos candle
From a modest home
Was all it took
To rouse a simple soul
Forever
We as girls
Can light a little candle
In our own homes
And that is all it takes
To spread light
Forever

Esther Korf, Age 15
Bais Chomesh Toronto
Ontario, Canada

> *My candle now ready to give, to create, inspire and share life.*

AN UNBROKEN CHAIN OF KINDNESS

I stand aside and watch my small flame,
I watch it shine aglow.
Looks so powerful, yet pure,
It just warms up my bones.

A majestic flame like a little princess,
So innocent and beautiful
Walks with dignity and grace,
Every step of hers so thoughtful.

This candle a fresh seed,
Learning and growing each day
Taking lessons from those near,
Till they're hard as clay.

Although I'm now on my own,
I still walk with warmth and pride;
My candle now ready to give,
To create, inspire and share life.

Racheli Dubov, Age 17
Bnos Menachem
Brooklyn, New York

Shabbat candles
Shabbos Candles, full of light
I can't wait until its night
Shimmer,
Sparkle,
Gleam and Shine
Thank goodness its soontime
Finally the day is done
Atlast the time has Come
For the Shabbat to arrive
To make our Souls feel alive
We Strike the match,
Scatch, Scrape, Scratch
We Say the Bracha
Baruch Atah
Because Hashem Commanded that
Lehadrick Neshel Shabbat.

SHABBAT CANDLES

Simcha Jacobs, Age 10

King David Primary School

Birmingham, England

I CAN DO IT

I can do it
I know no one else is interested
But I can do it
I know I haven't done it for years
But I can do it
I know my father won't approve of it
But I can do it
I know I forgot how to do it
But I can do it
I know my mother is no longer around to help me
But I can do it
I know I might be afraid
But I can do it
I know my siblings will be very angry with me
But I can do it
I know this might be the last thing I will do for my mother
But I can do it
I know everyone is against it
But I can do it
I know my mother will be watching me from up there and will help me
So I will do it just for her *neshama*
It seems very special
So I will do it

Mussy Engel, Age 14

Beth Rivkah Ladies College

Victoria, Australia

A MATCH OF INSPIRATION

The *Erev Shabbos* rush is behind me
I dress and take my place
I stand beside my candle
Let the peacefulness embrace.

Before I strike the match I think
I am just like it.
A girl without inspiration
Is like a match not lit.

I put the match to the box
And pull it, holding tight
The spark ignites, flame bursts forth
My fire burns tonight.

A lit match burns up quickly,
Act on that inspiration;
While it's burning, you're excited
But it's only on probation.

What will happen in some time,
When the fire flickers out?
Make it last, or let it die,
It's up to you to decide.

I take my match, and use it
I put it to my candle
Fire passes, wick flames up,
My inspiration I can handle.
I use it to light others
And to keep myself lit too
    This is the message of Shabbos candles:
        Share the light with one more Jew.

Ruth Davidov, Age 16
Bais Yaakov of Boston
Massachusetts, USA

> *A girl without inspiration is like a match not lit.*

MY SPECIAL CONNECTION

I love Shabbat because whenever I light my candle, I feel like I have a special connection with *Hashem*. Whenever I light my candle and cover my eyes, I feel like nothing in the world matters but only me and *Hashem*. I cover my eyes with my hands and wish that my family should always stay healthy and that all the bad things that happened that week should disappear for good. I would love to continue lighting my candle with my two sisters and blessing the whole world with only good and happiness.

Hodaya Sulliman-Zada, Age 12
Yeshiva Sha'arei Zion
New York, USA

♥ TIME TO REFLECT
YOUR JEWISH SOUL SHINING BRIGHTLY

Sit in a comfortable, relaxed position.
Close your eyes gently.
Take a deep breath in.

Breathe out slowly.
Take another breath in — 1,2,3.
Breathe out slowly — 1,2,3,4.

As you breathe deeply, release all the woes and worries of the week. Let all the tension fade away.

Feel lighter, as a soothing wave of relaxation flows over and through you. Visualize a candle before you. Take a match, strike it, and touch the wick gently. Coax it until the flame lights up on its own.

"*Ki Ner Hashem Nishmas Odom.*" The candle of G-d is the soul of man."
(King Solomon)

You are the Candle!
Your soul is the flame.
Your body is the wick.
You are lighting up the darkness.

When we ignite our Shabbos candle, we ignite our Jewish soul.
When we light the candle we connect to Hashem, we connect to the piece of G-d that is within us, we connect our loved ones to their holy spark within.

Breathe in *Hashem's* light — 1,2,3.
Hashem breathed a soul into you.
Allow your soul to shine. Allow yourself to connect to the Divine.
Breathe out — 1,2,3,4 and feel the glow of your inner flame.
Your Jewish soul is shining brightly.

Good Shabbos! Shabbat Shalom! Gut Shabbos!

❓ QUESTIONS TO CONSIDER

What special strength do you have inside you that's just waiting to shine?

This is your inner light. This is an expression of your soul that really wants to shine. Give yourself permission to shine today!

What mitzvah can you do today to shine?

A flame soars upward. Your soul is a flame!

How will you strive higher this Shabbos or this week?

Share your answers at www.JewishGirlsUnite.com.

CHAPTER 4:
Illuminating the Home

In this chapter, you will learn that the simple act of lighting Shabbos candles can light up your entire home! Did you know that when you take the time to gaze into the flame of your candles on Shabbos, you can see a light so bright, so powerful, that you can imagine it flowing throughout your entire home? We encourage you to take this extra moment to imagine the flame and its beauty throughout each room, each corner of the house.

STORY

NO ONE IS TOO SMALL TO LIGHT UP THE WORLD

New York was covered in snow. It was *Yud Shvat* 5734 - February 1974. I was four years old and had flown from London to New York with my mother and sister to visit the Rebbe. We prepared for our *yechidus*, our private meeting with the Rebbe.

Dressed in our Shabbos clothes, we waited in the antechamber, known as the *Gan Eden Hatachton*, with excitement and anticipation. And then we finally entered the Rebbe's room, the *Gan Eden Hoelyon*. There was a pure white light that seemed to radiate from the Rebbe's holy face. The scent of *kedusha* — of books and holiness — filled the room.

The Rebbe began to speak and said, "You are from London." I gasped as a thrill rushed through me. "How does the Rebbe know we are from London? *Ruach hakodesh*." I breathed in awe. We were in the presence of real *ruach hakodesh*, real Divine inspiration, a *tzaddik* like Moshe Rabbeinu!

The Rebbe gazed at us with blue eyes —כטוהר הרקיע— blue as the sky! It was a look that bore straight through to the soul and uplifted the heart with joy. This part I don't remember, but my mother tells how the Rebbe asked us how many times a day we say *Shema*. My older sister answered that we say *Shema* in the morning and the evening. The Rebbe said, "Very fine."

Now this *yechidus* took place in what I sometimes think of now as "the Dark Ages," in the days before it was common for little girls to

> *There was a pure white light that seemed to radiate from the Rebbe's holy face.*

> *"From Rivkah's example, we see what a young, three-year-old Jewish girl can do: She can kindle lamps which will radiate light for an entire week. Every little Jewish girl mirrors that light — by lighting candles every Friday, and before every festival."*
>
> *-The Lubavitcher Rebbe*

light Shabbos candles. The Rebbe first spoke publicly about the famous *Mivtzah Neshek* — Candle lighting Campaign — encouraging girls to add light to the world by lighting Shabbos candles in *Elul* 5734, nine months after this meeting with the Rebbe.

So what happened next was such a novelty that I remember it until today. The Rebbe told us that we should light Shabbos candles every week.

And of course we responded that we would!

Then the Rebbe spoke to my mother about her work, which is a fascinating story on its own. Hershel Pekkar, a talented silversmith who came originally from Russia and at that time was living in England, was on our flight back to London. He crafted for each of us a tiny silver candlestick.

The Rebbe blessing Rabbi Alexander and Leah before embarking to Sweden. The Rebbe said, (translated from Yiddish) "Chassidus says that a Yid must be freilach, joyful physically! You will be joyful and we will hear good news."

Upon our return to London, every time I would write to the Rebbe for a birthday, or before Rosh Hashanah or other special days, my father would remind me to tell the Rebbe that I was keeping my promise to light candles.

That tiny candlestick was placed on the table every week, together with my mother's own. Those included a pair of silver Shabbos candle-

Leah Namdar today teaching about the power of Jewish women.

sticks that my grandmother used to light and an old candlestick that my great-grandmother had used for Shabbos.

Every week, as I lit my new tiny candlestick together with my sister, I would close my eyes and remember how the Rebbe had told us to light candles to make the world a brighter place. How this candle was a link in the chain reaching back through the generations, connecting us with our past and creating our future, bringing *Moshiach* closer. And as I opened my eyes, the light that shone from that one little candle seemed to glow brighter and brighter, filling the whole house with its light.

> *The light that shone from that one little candle seemed to glow brighter and brighter.*

Years later, I realize that the Rebbe — in taking the time to give this beautiful instruction to two little girls — was giving over a profound message: **No one is too small to add more light to the world.**

Leah Namdar *and her husband Rabbi Alexander Namdar were sent by the Rebbe to Gothenburg, Sweden in 1991 to establish the first Chabad Center in Scandinavia, nurturing Jewish identity, education, and commitment. They are blessed with 11 children, thank G-d, and direct the Gan Israel Camps for children of European Chabad Shluchim.*

BRONZE PAGE

Bracha Chaya Katzenberg A"H

Our beloved mother was known for her
love of davening (prayer),
passion for kindness (Ahavas Yisroel), and
great care with Tznius.

She took the time to reach out to others
and inspire them to reach their potential.

May her Koach (strength) shine on us
as we continue to spread forth
her beautiful and altruistic legacy.

From her loving daughters:
Racheli Jacks ~ Ziva Katzenberg ~ Dina Tova Goldman

To our Precious Diamond Chayala,

Mazal Tov on becoming Bas Mitzvah! Wow, time flies so quickly, we were just davening for another child and then your light shone into our home and into our hearts. You made our world so much brighter and happier.

Our little Princess Chaya, you have now blossomed into a beautiful young woman shining your inner light and helping others. Chayala, we feel so blessed to have such a special daughter like you, your kindness always shines through. You are an amazing daughter and an amazing sister. You are a phenomenal little Balabuste and always help out for Shabbos. Whether it's cooking or baking or anything else we know we can count on you. You are always there to help.

Your name Chaya Sarah, is perfectly suited for you. Chaya, you are the symbol of hope, the symbol of life and the symbol of good mazal.* Sarah, with this name comes the three important mitzvos of a woman.

By now you know very well whom you were named after and of all the power your name gives you. Vehachay Yiten El Libo, and the living shall take to heart from the past Neshamos. You have the *Zechus Avos* of Savta Chaya Sara, Babby Gittel, Bubbe Chava, Bubby Leah and most recently Savta and Saba as well as all of our Helige family. You are benched with the Brachos of the Imahos especially Sara and have all the tools you need to succeed in life.

Now that you are Bas Mitzvah you have the opportunity to appreciate each mitzvah and do them with your whole heart, with simcha, and with chayus. May Hashem help you to have success in your studies and in your positive outlook.

You have the ability to influence your friends to do Chesed just like Savta with utmost Simchas Hachaim even when it seems difficult. When darkness surrounds you, use the light of Torah to guide you. Take this opportunity and use it in the most positive way, help shine away the darkness and help to bring Moshiach now!

We are so so proud of you and love you so much,

Mazal Tov!

LOVE,
ABBA AND MOMMY DONAT

Chaya Caras

MAY YOUR UNIQUE LIGHT
ALWAYS SHINE BRIGHTLY!

Love, Mommy & Tatty

🎵 SONG
AS THE SUN IS SETTING LOW

Lyrics by Chaviva Elharrar & Menucha Levin

As the sun is setting low
The Shabbos candles light aglow
I welcome in the Shabbos Queen
And with it a feeling serene

Chorus:
Lighting the candles so bright
It has so much power in this dark night
Touching my soul down deep within
What a special gift G-d has given

Connecting a nation so vast
One family united at last
A bond that can never break
The power that one small candle can make

Shabbos candles' special light
I'll kindle them every Friday night
The blessing I'll thank You above
For giving this mitzvah with love

OUR HUMBLE HOME

Sung by Chanale Fellig

Amongst the smiles
Amongst the tears
Of my childhood sweet and bitter years
There's a picture that my memory fondly frames
And through it shine two tiny flames

My mother's Shabbos candles
Which made our home so bright
Which faithfully she lighted
With a prayer on Friday night
And then around the table

We gathered and we heard
My father chant the *kiddush*
His heart in every word.

Our humble home became a mansion in that mystic glow
Our hearts were filled with hopes and dreams and thoughts of long ago
And still the tragic story of Israel's darkest nights
Has never dimmed the glory of my mother's Shabbos lights

Many of the songs in this book can be listened to at www.JewishGirlsUnite.com/songs.

CHAPTER 4: ILLUMINATING THE HOME

💬 GLOBAL VOICES

WELCOMING THE SHABBOS QUEEN

CHAOS TO CALM

Pots boiling on the stove
Papers scattered on the table
Rush, rush, the clock is ticking fast
Quick hide the laundry pile
Wipe up spills

I check the mirror
I pause
I breathe
Lift match to candle
Light flashes
Voice quiet
Whispering secret hopes
I smile at my daughters
Reach for a hug
Set the table
I can transform chaos into calm
Shabbos ends
Slowly back to noise and work
I feel my candle glow inside
When chaos creeps into my day
With fighting siblings
Friendships breaking
I can bring that Shabbos calm
Pause
And then share my flame of kindness
Smile, Listen, Laugh
Light someone else's candle
So they can pass it on

Mrs. Yedida Wolfe
JGU Writing Coach
Creative Online Club

IT FEELS LIKE HOME

A flicker in the night
The most magnificent light
Shines brilliantly everywhere
With tender loving care
When you light the candle
It feels like home
Finish and say
"Shabbat Shalom."

Sarah Berkowitz, Age 10
Beth Rivkah
New York, USA

GLOWING LIGHTS

The candlesticks wait there on the freshly set Shabbat table. The aroma of cooked food fills the air as the most amazing moment of the entire week approaches. My hand grasps the match and I swiftly give a strike, creating a force of empowering brightness. The penetrating light eradicates the darkness engulfing it and then subsides to a peaceful flame.

We, as Jewish women, have the power to usher in the holiness of Shabbat and embrace that time of tranquility, granting us a moment to breathe in the midst of our crazy weekly routines. I watch as my mother uses the three hand gestures to invite the Shabbat angels into our home and she covers her eyes with me. These are the few seconds I look forward to each week: moments to reflect on the past and pray to G-d for the awaiting steps of the future, and an auspicious time to connect to our Creator.

My hands slowly unfold to embrace my mother. I then gaze at the gentle glowing flames which always spread their warmth as the radiant candles seem to dance in their wicks. Happiness seeps through my body as the clocks of stress, errands, and work all seem to pause. The whole world joins to take a moment to appreciate the holiness of Shabbat. The creatures sing praises to G-d and throughout the streets, thousands of flames glow in unison.

Every week, regardless of what occurred or what will happen, we have an opportunity to perform a small but powerful action.

The legacy of our foremother, Sarah, continues to blaze through history as women worldwide light their special Friday night candle, all taking advantage of the incredible and uplifting opportunity we are blessed with.

The radiant candles seem to dance in their wicks.

Brocha Chaya Jacks, Age 15
Beth Rivkah Ladies College
Melbourne, Australia

LIGHTING A CANDLE

Lighting a candle is like lighting a person's life with Torah, *mitzvot*, and kindness. It is also like making the person spread the Torah and *mitzvot* to everyone else, even non-religious people.

Maggie Hakin, Age 8
Beth Rivkah School
Melbourne, Australia

MY CANDLESTICK

When I was three years old, I started lighting Shabbos candles because the Rebbe said that this was a special mitzvah for Jewish girls to bring *kedusha* (holiness) to the world.

I loved Shabbos so much when I was little that I used to cry when Shabbos was coming to an end because I knew I would have to wait a whole week for Shabbos to come again. I also got really excited every Friday because I knew later that evening I would be able to bring *kedusha* when I lit my candle, and have so much Shabbos left to spend with my family.

My very own Shabbos candle was given to me by my *Bubby* from South Africa. I love it because it is one of a kind. It doesn't match my mommy's candles or look like my older sister's candlestick either. It has pretty silver designs and is nice and tall. I am grateful that it is so beautiful.

To this day, I get so excited when we polish the candlesticks. I feel a special connection to Shabbos because Shabbos is the seventh (*sheva*) day of the week and my name, Elisheva has the word *sheva*, in it. I still look forward to Shabbos, but don't cry when it ends anymore. Unlike holidays like Rosh Hashanah and Purim, Shabbos is always just a week away. For seven years I have been enjoying and beautifying the mitzvah of lighting Shabbos candles and look forward to watching my flames flicker and grow each week.

Elisheva Trapedo, Age 10
Teaneck New Jersey School
New Jersey, USA

ONE SMALL FLAME

On Friday night
A small flame's light
Fills my home with glow
The red sun drops
And all work stops
"It's Shabbos," all Jews know.

When shadows fall
For help we call
One small flame breaks the night
We'll never see
The sheer beauty
Of one flame's shining light.

Outside rain pours
And a harsh wind roars
Yet no one seems to care
The whole world sings
Despite the winds
"Shalom Aleichem" fills the air.

On Friday night
Our candlelight
Is a torch for all to see
And every part
Brightens the heart
Inside of you and me.

Chaya M. Mandel, Age 11

Shluchim Online School
Texas, USA

SHABBOS IS THE BEST

Shabbos, Shabbos is the best,
It's the day *Hashem* did rest.
The world was finished on that day,
We should treat it a special way.

Those who treat it with respect,
Hashem will surely pay you back.
You'll be protected, that I know,
Shabbos *Kodesh*, I love you so.

I lit the candles which burned so bright,
They still kept burning all through the night.
Just as candles shine so bright,
The Torah will also hold us tight.

Avital Pleshtiyev, Age 10

Yeshiva Sha'arei Zion
New York, USA

J'AIME ALLUMER

Moi Kiara, j'ai aimé allumer les bougies de Chabbat. J'ai aimé parce que c'est beau d'allumer les bougies de Chabbat.

I, Kiara, light a Shabbat candle. I love to light Shabbat candles because it's beautiful!

Kiara Esther Benvenuto, Age 8

Talmud Torah
St. Denis, France

SO VERY BRIGHT

The Shabbat candles so very bright
I light them every Friday night
So beautiful, so nice
It makes me happy each time I light
The Shabbat candles so very bright

Bassie Rubin, Age 10

Maimonides Hebrew Day School
New York, USA

A SHABBAT CANDLE LIGHT

A candle brings light to a house, but a Shabbat candle brings life to us. Mama lights the candles and prays to *Hashem*. One day I'll do the same. When Mama talks to *Hashem*, she asks Him for health and happiness for me and my brothers. When we have Shabbat with the candles, it brings Shabbat to life. The candle flames dance around, and when the light is gone in the morning, I can't wait for the next Shabbat so we can light again.

Rebecca Kharasov, Age 12

Yeshiva Sha'arei Zion
New York, USA

THE GOLDEN LINK

Ever since I started lighting Shabbat candles, I have felt a special connection, a connection between me and *Hashem*. I feel the peace and serenity going throughout the whole house. I know that I have extra time to *daven* for those in need.

Every time I light candles, I am reminded of my job and place in the world. I know that I am now part of the golden link in the chain, connecting the whole world.

As I circle my hands three times, I think of *Hashem's* amazing world. I push out the darkness physically and mentally. All the things that I thought were bad in the week, melt away. All stress is gone. I light Shabbat candles. I feel relaxed. I feel peace in the house. Shabbat candles are truly a miracle.

Ellie Posner, Age 11

Bader Hillel Academy
Wisconsin, USA

> *A candle brings light to a house, but a Shabbat candle brings life to us.*

SHABBOS CANDLE LIGHTING

Friday rushed by
Full of running and cooking
And cleaning and baking
Food in the oven
So many smells that I'm lovin'
Shower was taken
I'm dressed in Shabbos fashion.

I'm beckoned on over
A nickel dropped in my hand
Put in the *pushkah*
For peace in the land.

I strike the match quickly
But it doesn't light
I try once again,
And then it ignites.

I guide my shimmering key
Into the lock of my candle
It creates a towering flame
Reaching up toward G-d
As if to proclaim
His Heavenly name.

I gather in its light,
Then cover my eyes with
My hand-made veil
And pray to the One Above
Who's listening —
So full of love.

A heavenly presence descends
A door opens wide
To reveal a time to transcend
Above the worldly tide.

With one little action
I brought in Shabbos
The Queen I welcome
My home now a palace.

With grace she enters
And I shiver
And then my hands part to reveal
a small little flame,
So innocent and surreal.

It seems to brighten
The impending night
And I stare at it
Transfixed. Transformed.

Chaya Eber, Age 15
Ohel Chana School
California, USA

BEHIND MY COVERED EYES

Some time before the evening sun begins to wane,
Hectic running makes it feel as though the minutes are passing
Quicker than any other time.
As soon as I cover my eyes to *bentch* my Shabbos candle,
Beautiful Shabbos light spreads its wings over our house.
By fulfilling the special mitzvah that *Hashem* gave to girls,
Our requests gain an extra power when we ask *Hashem*,
Show us the light of Paradise now!

Mussie Yehudah, Age 12
Bais Chaya Mushka
Iowa, USA

I AM AGLOW

As the week goes by,
I sit in the tall glass cupboard untouched;
Then Friday comes around,
And I am clutched.
I feel excited as the warm cloth brushes down my back;
I receive a special treat
The soft polish from the pack.
I am placed on a tray, as silver as can be,
On display
For all to see.
Then I am lit to spread some light,
I am aglow,
That is hard to fight;
As I watch everyone bask in my light,
It is a beautiful scene,
A magnificent sight.
I have watched Shabbos for so many years,
Through times of laughter,
And times of tears.
Even though I will burn out,
I know Shabbos will come again without a doubt.

Esther Groner, Age 11
Beth Rivkah Ladies College
Melbourne, Australia

THREE SPARKLING CANDLES

Three sparkling candles just for me and Mom because we are keeping Shabbat. We love in our heart as we light. We are Shabbat angels in skirts. We are happy because we are keeping Shabbat. Shabbat is almost over. We do *Havdala*.
Shabbat Shalom!

Brayden Yona Gross, Age 7
Southern Connecticut Hebrew Academy
Connecticut, USA

CAMP SHABBOS

As I walk to the camp dining room, I look ahead and see all the girls, part of the sleep-away camp Pardes Chana, milling around the table filled with tea-lights for the girls to light. The very first Shabbos in camp I suddenly feel a wave of homesickness, wishing I was back home in New Jersey with my family instead of up in Montreal. Then I feel a new feeling — a feeling of calmness, peacefulness, and a feeling of happiness. I walk to the table to light. When I finish, I walk to my sister to give her a Shabbos hug.

Rochele Goldenberg, Age 12
Cheder Menachem
New Jersey, USA

SHABBOS KODESH

As the wick is caught
With the fiery flame
Peacefulness descends
Shabbos Kodesh is its name.

Each Friday night
When the match is lit
The wick and fire hold hands
And together they commit.

Into this home
They will bring peace
And *Shalom Bayis*
The candles will
increase.

The fire grows in size
And dances merrily in
the light,
Its excited spark and gleam
Can illuminate the night.

The light from the candles
Will the family surround
And joy will be heard
Echoing all around.

The world was made in six days,
On the seventh G-d did rest;
And so it is this day
That we designate for the best.

A woman that kindles
These lights so joyfully
Will merit long life
For her whole family.

The Talmud expounds that,
In addition to her earning,
Her sons and sons-in-law
Will be rewarded in their learning.

When the angels enter
And see the candles ablaze,
The good one will bless and
The bad one will add more
praise.

The ultimate light of
Moshiach,
The *Midrash* does write,
is brought on by Shabbos
Through the candles that we
ignite.
Good Shabbos!

> *The wick and fire hold hands*

Rivka Goldberg, Age 14
Bais Rivkah High School
New York, USA

WHAT BRINGS LIGHT, BRINGS HOPE

A woman looks ahead,
Tears glistening in her eyes,
Gives a whispering prayer
And bursts then into cries.

Why the misery? Why the sadness?
Tears trickling down her face,
Why the bloodshed, pain and sickness?
...The world's an evil place.

Yet one more spark was there,
A fire burning low,
The *davening* it did hear;
In the dingy room it glowed.

The peaceful little flame
Bringing the Shabbos in
Listened to the quiet sobs
And yearned to do something.

But it was just a candle;
Its power, to bring light
To our soul in the hardest times,
To shine with all its might.

So as the woman wept and prayed,
The flame just grew and grew,
Crying out in its own way:
There's so much good to do!

A wonderful warmth
And beautiful light
Soon lit up the whole house;
Tears dried up,
Peace regained,
The Blessings were recited
And the holiness remained.

"...*Lehadlik Ner shel Shabbos Kodesh*."
Because what brings light, brings hope!

Leah Myers, Age 12
Israeli Shluchim Online School
Bratislava, Slovakia

CANDLE LIGHTING

Every Friday night I light Shabbos candles with my mom. It's my job to set up five candles for my mom and one for me. I put a *tichel* on. I cover my eyes and say a *bracha*. I thank *Hashem* for all the great gifts He gives me. I always make sure that I light on time, and sometimes I even light early. I am so proud to be a Jewish girl.

Rebeccah Forti, Age 7
Southern Connecticut
Hebrew Academy
Connecticut, USA

KINDLE THE LIGHT!

Shabbos candles, light 'em and you'll see,
Peacefulness at home, utmost serenity.

Identity, Jewish;
The light in the world lost; the darkness penetrates,
And by lighting these lights, we rekindle the misplaced,
Those wandering souls who are searching for who they are,
Their purpose on this earth,
Groping from afar.

On the first day G-d said, "Good,"
So from then on women would
Light the Shabbos candle
To shatter the darkness
That the world 'til now withstood,
Adding to the harsh, bitter cold, the good.

We, the women, kindle this light
To right the wrong that Chava had done,
By the sin of the tree of knowledge
And brought the world darkness and fright
By extinguishing G-d's candle,
Without which the dark world could not handle.

Because we set with love the tone,
We are the foundation of the home;
And when it comes to adding light, we are the ones to increase and deepen,
Since it is us, at home, from where spirituality does begin.

On Shabbos we have an extra light,
An extra soul,
And with this we fill the deep, musty, empty hole
That will be in our hearts
'til the final redemption,
When G-d will not make even one exception.

So until then, let's unify,
And the Shabbos we will beautify,
By getting one more special soul
To kindle the light on the holy Friday night.
So grab this opportunity to light up the world,
And when we close our eyes to ask for blessings,
Let us all pray that the final redemption comes today!

Zelda Shwarzberg, Age 13
Bais Rivkah
New York, USA

> *On Shabbos we have an extra light, an extra soul.*

THE CLOCK DOESN'T WAIT

Rush, charge
Live life in a hurry
Race against time
The clock doesn't wait

Wipe, dust
Clear the world around you
Washing, cleansing
The clock doesn't wait

Arrive, depart
From one place to the next
Darting, flashing
The clock doesn't wait

Work, toil
Six days a week
Striving, climbing
The clock doesn't wait

Friday night
Hold time in its place
Take a moment to light
The clock can wait

Feel the glow
The radiance, the warmth
As it opens your mind
Releases your soul

A fire, a flame
Ignite a soul
Light up the world
By doing your part

Just one moment
Just one light
Just one deed
Makes a world of a difference

Fraida Blau, Age 15
Beis Chaya Mushka
New York, USA

DANCING FLAMES

Pulling Shabbos with each hand
Three times together
While you stand

It bursts to flame
Golden warmth
Flickering upwards — never tame

A time to hope
A time to wish
Cleaning worries — bar of soap

Dancing flames bring light
Brighten up your meal
Throughout the night

The wax drips away
Until nothing is left
Start of a new day

But worry not
Because next week again
You light — your candles won't rot

And you can watch as —
Your candle bursts to flame
Golden warmth
Flickering upwards — never tame

Moussia Lew, Age 12
Bnos Menachem School, New York USA

TURN TO GREET THE SHABBOS QUEEN

As I strike a match and kindle a flame, I feel a sense of joy. This fire is like any other, yet it stands apart. A fire of any size, be it a raging inferno or a single match, has inside it strength. Strength to destroy that which is weak, a passion to burn what stands in its way. Due to this, people tend to dislike fire; yet each week we create a flame within our homes.

Of course, we have a reason. The tiny, dancing wicks help to kindle the flame within each of us, and connect us to *Hashem*. As we light those flames, we are reminded of all that they represent and of the Shabbos Queen who is so graciously welcomed into our homes each Friday night. Because when the Shabbos *neiros* are lit, they shine so brightly that the whole world basks in their glory. With a smile on my face, I light two candles and turn to greet the Queen.

Devorah Gold, Age 14
Bais Yaakov High School
Indiana, USA

♀ TIME TO REFLECT
WELCOME THE SHABBOS QUEEN

Make yourself comfortable as you sit in a relaxed position.
Take a deep breath in.
Breathe out slowly.
Take another breath in. Count 1,2,3.
Breathe out slowly. Count 1,2,3,4.

Gaze at your Shabbos candle's flame. This tiny flame illuminates your home and heart.
Let your candle pierce the darkness.
Notice a feeling of calm as Shabbos enters your home.

Breathe in the sweet aroma of Shabbos.
Breathe in the aroma of the nourishing chicken soup.
Breathe in the aroma of the heavenly challah.
Breathe in the aroma of truth and tranquility.

Come out my Beloved, the Bride to meet;
The inner light of Shabbat, let us greet.

Lecho Dodi, Enter O Bride, enter O Bride;
O Bride, Shabbos Queen, now come here!

You smile and welcome the Shabbos Queen, a perfect embodiment of beauty. Her appearance is royal and elegant. Feel her nurturing and caring presence.

Can you feel the healing? Can you feel the love?

Let a feeling of security and serenity surround you.

The room is so bright, full of light and *kedusha*. Breathe it in — it will soothe your soul.

❓ QUESTIONS TO CONSIDER

Women and girls usher in the light and warmth of Shabbos into our homes and hearts. We connect the souls of our family with the Divine light of Shabbos.

Describe the transformation that takes place in your home and heart when you light Shabbos candles.

How do you welcome the Shabbos Queen?

Share your answers at www.JewishGirlsUnite.com.

CHAPTER 5:
Transforming the Darkness

In this chapter, you will learn that you have the power to transform your dark moments into light. Did you know that when you feel a dark thought, or anything negative, you can use your breath to break that negative feeling and intentionally look for a more positive outlook? With commitment and intention, you can use the act of lighting your Shabbos candles as a physical manifestation of creating light in your life! Light the match — see how it makes your space glow! Use that glow to find your positive thoughts.

STORY

LONGING FOR THE LIGHT

The Shabbos table was beautifully set with my mother's delicious homemade challah and gourmet Sephardic cooking. My father, Rabbi Azriel Yitzchok Wasserman O"BM was smiling, surrounded by a table filled with guests. I was eight years old and loved singing along with my father and listening to his dynamic storytelling at the Shabbos meal. Everyone loved him and wanted to learn from him. He was a beloved teacher for young and old, a beacon of light, inspiring everyone with his wisdom and passion. My parents' home sparkled with *kedusha* and provided a haven to those lacking family and community.

My world was engulfed in darkness at age ten, when I lost my father and teacher. I missed him terribly and soaked my pillow with tears. Now, I was the girl without a father and felt judged by others. I yearned to hear my father chant the *kiddush* on Friday night with joy in every word. My home and my heart felt incomplete.

As the oldest and only girl, I felt responsible to help my dear mother with a newborn baby (named after my father) and my two younger brothers. We found ourselves on the receiving end of the kindness of wonderful people in the Crown Heights, Brooklyn community.

During my teenage years and on, I craved to celebrate Shabbos and Holidays at my father's table illuminated by his wisdom and love. I longed to learn from him and bask in his light. I struggled with buried emotions of pain and grief for over 30 years. The grief did not go away and every so often it would whisper, "I'm still here."

My dear friend and coach Susan encouraged me to reflect on several crucially significant questions:

What if I could let go of the pain and sadness and replace it with my beloved father's love and light? What if I could rejoice in being the

Nechama Dina at age 4 with her father, Rabbi Azriel Yitzchok Wasserman OB"M

Nechama Dina with her family today at her oldest daughter's wedding.

daughter of an incredible person, who touched me during the formative years of my life? What if I could dedicate a legacy project to his loving memory and connect to his soul?

I finally understood that I had the choice to get lost in the darkness or search for the concealed light.

Aishes Chayil Mi Yimtza, A Woman of Valor who can find?" The words we sing every Friday night spoke to me in a personal way. I wanted to discover my true self, free from being weighed down by the feelings of painful loss.

Was that even possible? Where would I find the strength?

"All it takes is one small candle to dispel darkness."

I asked people who had known my father to share their memories with me. The stories about his life touched me deeply. As a result of all this, my soul connected to my father's legacy. I felt his love and joy flow into my aching heart, and his light began to shine in my life once again. When I lit my Shabbos candles, I prayed for comfort and an open heart to receive the strength I needed to heal and overcome internal darkness. Sarah *Imeinu's* candles became my source of light and blessing. They reminded me each week that I have been given the power to turn pain into purpose and transform the darkness.

I made a conscious choice to see and appreciate the light instead of focusing on darkness. I took the time to reflect, to journal, to express gratitude, to cry, to pray, to sing, and to let go of the pain. I dedicated my life to creating a global community of empowered girls as a fitting legacy for my father. When I share his teachings, my heart is filled with joy because I know that he will always be remembered. The light of his legacy pierced through the pain in my wounded 10-year-old heart.

I finally understood that the light that emerges from darkness is so much greater than ordinary light. Today, I find my beloved father's light in the blessing of my husband and ten children KA"H. I find my father's light when I comfort a young girl's grieving heart. I find my father's light when I teach women and girls. I find my father's light in the loving Shabbos atmosphere at JGU retreats. And most of all, I find my father's light shining through me.

And when I spent *Simchat Torah* in *Maarat Hamachpela* with my Bat Mitzvah daughter Rivkah, in the place where our Matriarchs Sarah and Rivkah lit their Shabbos candles, I finally felt whole and complete inside. It was there that I had a revelation that no matter what darkness we face, the light of our ancestors still shines and gives us the strength to shine our inner light. I thank *Hashem* and all those who have guided me on my journey to find *Nechama* — comfort — and my true self.

Nechama Dina Laber *is the JGU Founder & Global Director and the Founder of the Jewish Girls Retreat. She is a Professional Speaker, Personal Mentor and Judaic Educational Consultant. She is the Chabad representative to Southern Rensselaer County with her husband, Rabbi Avraham Laber, and their ten children KA"H.*

> *I made a conscious choice to see and appreciate the light instead of focusing on darkness.*

GOLD PAGE

Nechama Dina's picture in "A Candle of My Own" book at age 5

Nechama Dina with the JGU Global Leadership Team at the 2016 Anniversary Celebration

I have a vision of the Rebbe leafing through the second candle lighting book, *A Candle Of My Own*, and smiling at my photograph. The Rebbe's gaze still inspires me to empower our Jewish daughters to light their own candle, and discover their own unique gifts to illuminate the world!

As a young girl, from across the sparkling Shabbos table, I watched my mother deep in prayer; she was our beautiful Shabbos queen. I learned to love Shabbos and couldn't wait to light my own candle.

Today, I have transformed these early experiences from my childhood into my own home and into my work with Jewish women and girls. I feel blessed and thank Hashem for the privilege of being part of the vital mission to establish future Jewish homes and help our Jewish daughters become Jewish mothers.

—Nechama Dina

"Nechama Dina Wasserman Laber is a leader with great vision! She is able to see the goal and big picture of Jewish growth and unity and at the same time never misses caring for every single individual. Her warmth and generous sharing touch the hearts of those she meets. Her courage and constant faith and joy are a real inspiration. May Hashem bentch you, dearest Nechama, to keep on lighting up hearts and homes around the world."

With love, Leah Namdar, Co-Director of Chabad of Sweden

SPONSORED BY JGU PARENTS IN HONOR OF NECHAMA DINA WASSERMAN LABER'S LOVE AND LEADERSHIP OF OUR JEWISH DAUGHTERS.

Warrior of Light

Bubby Breindel Cziment

A loving tribute from your granddaughter Nechama Dena Zwiebel

Five generations of women and girls kindling the flames each Friday night.

My grandmother, having just turned Bas Mitzva, was faced with a life altering choice,

She decided to listen to her innermost self, her pure neshama, her life- affirming voice.

Courageously, she made the decision that she must survive!

Her distinguished family's legacy must continue to thrive!

In the forest, one night, her late grandfather appeared.

"Eat whatever you see to survive; the Germans are always to be feared.

If you see them, they will not see you; if you don't, keep an eye and even hide.

Now look up." He finished. She saw fish swimming in clear blue water, their eyes open wide.

This was the first of many moments of light, in the darkest of darkest times for the Jews.

Her eyes were opened to ongoing miracles, and each time for her to live, Hashem did choose.

Her trials continued even after the war's end, when her husband of just several short years became ill.

He had worked in the coal mines during the war, and its devastating toxicity affected him still.

Widowed, a couple of years later, and left with 6 mouths to feed, she again shone light into darkness.

Her skills as a seamstress which she had used to survive, she would once again harness.

Through challenging times, joyful occasions, or just to connect with the Master of the Universe,

She would be found with a Tehillim in hand and her sweet sincere voice, enunciating each word.

When amongst other survivors, she chose to focus on gratitude, for the brochos she had been given.

When beset with tests, she publicly displayed a shining example of trust in Hashem to all Yidden.

She was a courageous warrior of light, maintaining her dignity and her strong commitment to her family.

Her children have continued to be Ambassadors Of Light, each in his/her respective community.

As the twilight of her life beckoned, 5 generations of first born girls, gathered together as she proclaimed,

"This is my sweetest retaliation- a large observant family glorifying Hashem's name!"

I am one of those first born girls, a third generation survivor, continuing my Grandmother's legacy of light.

I'm committed to restore the light of 6 million souls, through 6 million new flames on Friday night.

Her 90 fulfilling years on this earth are a testimony to the Jewish woman's inner and outer sovereignty.

I invite you to commit to introduce women far and wide, to the Shabbos light prayer and tranquility.

Together we can reach the goal of 6 million new flames rising up on high to the Heavenly throne.

May we hear the Heavenly proclamation, "Beloved Jewish Women, you have built My third Eternal Home!"

HENYA BAS AHARON YOSEF O"BM
Yahrzeit 9th of Menachem Av

Dear Ma, Your light shines on

Precious Gem

I lost a precious gem
A precious jewel
You were my tool
To understand life
To help me in my strife
Now what am I to do?

I feel your love from above,
And see your smile
From a mile
Away
Your life illuminates mine
Your love illuminates my life and transcends me above my strife

Beloved Ma,
Your light shines on here in this world, forever and ever, we feel your love from above, and may we always be blessed to feel you in our lives! Love, your family!

♪ SONG
SHINE A LITTLE LIGHT

Composed by Yitzi Hurwitz
With blessings for good news

Can't you see
I'm trying to be
All that you
Want of me?

But it's so cold now
It's so dark here
What could I do?
It's not very clear

Chorus:
Shine a little light
Show us the way
Lead us to
A brighter day
(Repeat)

If I'm a little light,
You're a little light
Together we are
So very bright

A little light here
A little light there
See the smiles
It's so very clear

Chorus:
Shine a little light
Show us the way
Lead us to
A brighter day
(Repeat)

When we stand together as one
There's nothing that we can't do,
So let's lead the way
To a brighter day
And the whole world will join along.

We can bring a brighter day
For everyone,
It's only up to me and you
We can see it, we all believe it,
So let us shine our light right now.

Chorus:
Shine a little light
Show us the way
Lead us to
A brighter day
(Repeat)

WOMEN OF THE FUTURE

Composed at the Jewish Girls Retreat by Mali New

Here I stand today
Paving my own way
Just like Sara, I will too
Touch the soul of every Jew

Leah changed the norm
Went out to transform
How, *Hashem*, can I be like them?

There's more there than it seems
Take Esther, who was queen
Devorah judged beneath a tree
Left her home so modestly

I'll run that extra mile
Show the world my style
I yearn to be a true *Aishes Chayil*

Time and time again
The power of us women
We can shine our inner lights

It's in our hands today
Spread forth the holy way
How can I be a *Shlucha*?
How can I be a Leader?

Chorus:
Women of the future
Now is your chance to
See your greater strength unfurl
Shove away the darkness
You have the power to
Bring day to the world

Many of the songs in this book can be listened to at www.JewishGirlsUnite.com/songs.

💬 GLOBAL VOICES

FROM DARKNESS TO LIGHT

CHANGE THE WORLD!

One little Shabbos candle can chase away a lot of darkness
One little Shabbos candle can help someone find the way
One little Shabbos can change the world
You can change sadness to happiness

You can bring an innocent child back home
You can change the world
Can you unite the spark? You decide.

Mariasha Malka Schtroks, Age 11
Shluchim Online School
British Columbia, Canada

GOOD WILL COME

I'm sure no one desires
Sadness, hurt, and pain
And I can light the world up now
And stop the endless strain.

I raise my eyes and *daven*,
I smile knowingly,
I'm sure that good will come of this
If only they light me.

A match comes closer, closer
A flame lights up the air
My soul soars up much higher,
A candle now is there.

Rivka Resnick, Age 12
Lubavitcher Yeshiva Academy
Massachusetts, USA

CANDLES BURNING

Candles burning,
Lives are turning,
Each one a flame
With a separate name.

One spark lights up
Another's life,
Helping them through,
Sorrow and strife.

Shabbos candles,
With their special light,
Shine upon the world
Every Friday night.

Moussie Mandel, Age 11
Bnos Menachem, New York, USA

MY CANDLES FOREVER

I bring my hands toward me, the wrinkles she does see —
My darkened number on my arm for all eternity.
A soul so pure and precious, to evil she is not wise,
And the candles that shine before her create a hope that never dies.
My tears flow on her shoulder; as she becomes aware,
She notices my broken heart and questions me with care.
How can I answer such a child, to whom life is unknown,
Whose knowledge is so limited of the horrors that were shown?
I wipe away the tears as the memories blur my mind;
I know she wants an answer, and these are the words I find:
When I was young and just like you, they hated all the Jews;
They wanted to get rid of me, but truth I had to choose.
Every Friday when sunset came, I knew the time was near
For me to light the candles, amidst all of the fear.
We were beaten, starved and whipped, lives torn apart each day,
But those candlesticks remained with me; how I prayed that they would stay!
I never lost those candles — they were always by my side,
I was a Jewish girl, and my faith I'd never hide.
Although my family is now gone — they were killed before my eyes —
The candles are my source of light throughout my trying times.
My candles are my guidance; they are my streetlights in the dark;
As I make my way through saddest days, they add that extra spark.
They remind me of the evil men who wanted to take my life,
Yet I lit those Shabbos candles at those moments of great strife.
My dearest one, it may be hard, but to yourself you must be true —
You are a daughter of *Hashem*, a very special Jew.

Golda Epstein, Age 16
Yeshiva Girls School of Pittsburgh
Pennsylvania, USA

A BRIGHTER PLACE

When I lit my first light
On that wintry Friday night,
I wondered how it could be
That the world could be brighter
By that little candle
Lit by me?
I thought about how many
candles in the world
there might be,
Maybe two million
and two;
Now with my candle,
Two million and three!
So now my friends,
light will never end.
It will stay forever
No matter the weather.
From the moment I turned three,
The world was brighter because of ME.
Now you have the chance to do the same
When you do the mitzvah of igniting the flame.
When all the lights join together
It's when *Moshiach* will surely come!
I can't wait to see with my eyes
The light that was added from this candle of mine.

Mussi Benjaminson, Age 9

Cheder Lubavitch Morristown

New Jersey, USA

LIFE WITHOUT SHABBOS

When I try to imagine a life without Shabbos, I panic.
I see meetings and homework, tournaments and responsibilities
Crowding their way into every day of my life.
I see my calendar filled so full
I write spaces for breathing each day.
I see myself collapsing
from pressure, strain, and fatigue.
I see myself failing, because
I have no calm and no time for me.
Shabbos is my glue, reapplied
every week to the broken shards that form my chaotic world.
Shabbos is my air bubble, letting me breathe as I drown in the sea of life.
Shabbos is my light at the end of the tunnel, guiding me through the darkness of the week.
Shabbos is my peace.
I could not survive without Shabbos.

Tamar Dimbert, Age 17

Hanna Sacks Bais Yaakov

Illinois, USA

> *Shabbos is my light at the end of the tunnel.*

THE BATTLE OF LIGHT

Darkness permeating the air
Engulfing, drawing in
Dejection and despair;
So began the beginning.
But with a mighty command
The void was filled with light
Insects swarmed the land
The moon brought on the night.
With each day of creation
Myriads of sparks spread wide
Hashem's perfect imperfection
For man to live inside.
The flames spread high and low
Holiness in its prime
Setting the world aglow
The light of eternal time.
Yet one action is all it took
Shattering the paradisaical bliss
For the taste of forbidden fruit
Is a taste too hard to resist.
So Chava began her fight
The never-ending scheme
To re-attain the distinguished light
And re-crown the desired dream.
Each week she did the same
Spreading more and more light
Kindling her flames
'Lehadlik'- she would ignite.
And deep within our hearts
Is the key to fulfill this task
To help rekindle the spark
That rests beneath its mask.
From age three, every week, each Jewish girl
Is granted this sacred mission
Let me tell you — you're not the first!
This links on for generations.
Sara *Imeinu's* candles, each day
Burned bright for all to see
She strengthened a link in the chain
Passing on this sacred deed.
And all through the years
The tradition has followed through
During hardship, war or fear
The flames of Shabbos were still in view.
From the depths of exile in Spain
To the heights of English hills
Through the terror of a Russian train
The flames burned stronger still.
In peace, in happiness, in war,
No matter the time or place
The Shabbos lights, I'm sure,
Will be lit and blessed with grace.
And *'Bizchut Nashim Tzidkaniyut'*
In the merit of our righteousness
We'll be redeemed from our *galut*
And the world will be aflame with holiness.

Esther Miriam Golomb, Age 16
Leeds Jewish High School For girls
Leeds, United Kingdom

A FLICKERING FLAME

A flickering flame
A dancing light
A glowing spark
A beautiful sight

One small candle
To unveil the illusion
One small lamp
To give us that infusion

All around the globe
Girls and women light
Illuminating the world
Lighting up the night

A blazing fire
Now ignited
To bring *Moshiach*
When we will all be reunited

Mushka Rodal, Age 14
Beis Rebbe
California, USA

SPREADING LIGHT

Shabbos candles means to me that it glows when I light it. That it is a mitzvah because I light saying the *bracha* and give everyone a kiss and say Good Shabbos. When I light the candles, it spreads the light all over the world and people come and they light Shabbos candles with us. And I love putting a lot of money in the *pushka* more than once, because I just love looking at the poor people because I like to give them money and food.

Shayna Nemtzov, Age 6
Lamplighter Jewish Academy
California, USA

READY FOR THE LIGHT

During each Friday night there was darkness in the streets,
The only light for miles was in the Jewish homes.
It looks like *Moshiach* this time,
Can't wait for the special time to shine.
Don't mess with our glow cause we'll get you every time.
Then the candles lit,
Brighter than ever before,
Won't let them fade,
This candle meant for much more.
During each Friday night I could finally see,
I knew the day would come and I would go to my home country.
It looks like now's the time
That we should stand up for the fight,
This darkness is over and I'm ready for the light.

Neshama Sari, Age 12
Homeschool/Jewish Online School
Oregon, USA

ONE CANDLE

One strike of a match
In a very dark place,
You can illuminate it
And put a smile on a face.
When each person lights just one candle
In a very dark world
There are thousands of candles
To brighten up the world.

Chana Backman, Age 12
Beis Rebbe
California, USA

JUST ONE LITTLE CANDLE

I'm just one little candle in a big world
Of what difference am I?
One day I was put on a candlestick and I wanted to cry.
All I do is burn, as I fade away;
To the young girl in front of me I finally did say:
"What are you doing to me,
Are you lighting me so I'll melt down?
I've always wanted to know the reason," and then ended with a frown.
As I stood that evening, when I was almost done,
Her words played in my head — I remember every one:
"As I kindle you tonight, a mitzvah you help me do
For as I kindle you tonight, a blessing I say on you.
You help welcome Shabbos in with your flame so bright,
This Friday night you got the chance to share with the world your light.
And though you are small, you make the biggest difference of all.
Because this world is so dark, we need your special spark
And if every week all the girls in my class would light one of your friends
Moshiach would come, for this darkness would end!"

Mushka Heidingsfeld, Age 12
Simcha Monica
California, USA

A LIGHT THAT BRIGHTENS

A flame flickers
Furiously flurrying into the night
Amid the darkness
It's a light
A light that brightens
Up the night
There goes the flame
Rising above it all
A burning sensation
That is created

Chanah Lew, Age 18
New York, USA

A WOMAN OF VALOR

As a Jewish girl, I feel privileged that I was entrusted with the mitzvah of welcoming Shabbos each week. On Friday night, we sing the *Aishet Chayil* – Who can find a woman of valor? What does the word "*Chayil*" mean? "*Chayil*" means "soldier." The woman of valor is a determined individual who faces the world's great darkness and challenges with courage and strength. What are her weapons? In Hebrew *neshek* means weapons. The *Nun Shin Kuf* is an acronym for "*Neirot Shabbat Kodesh*." The Shabbat candle is an "*Aishet Chayil's*" weapon of light to fight darkness. We fight with light and we will win!

One of the reasons why *Hashem* gave the mitzvah of lighting Shabbos candles to women is because when *Hashem* redeemed us from Egypt the women were the "beacons of light" who gave encouragement to their husbands and assured them that *Hashem* would not forsake His people. They continued to have children and build Jewish homes through the darkest moments in time. So too, in our generation the women spread light and hope and are the source of the Jewish people's staunch belief in the final Redemption, and in their merit *Moshiach* will come.

Shaina Laber, Age 12
Maimonides Hebrew Day School
New York, USA

SHABBOS CANDLES

Shabbos is here,
It's candle lighting time,
Into the *pushka* I drop my dime.
I strike my match, it does ignite,
Then my Shabbos candle I light.
I move my hands in circles three
Then cover my eyes very gently;
Lehadlik Ner Shel Shabbos Kodesh,
With this *bracha* the candles I bless.
We welcome the Shabbos Queen each Friday night
With our candles that make the world bright.
I look at the candles
My heart filled with love,
Full of thanks to *Hashem*, the One Above!

Chana Simpson, Age 11
Shluchim Online School
Ohio, USA

CANDLELIGHT

Serenity and peace surrounding me
Happiness in the air
A special island of time
Breaking through challenges of the week
Bringing light into the world
One candle at a time
Shabbos- I anxiously await you the whole week through

Malkie Fox, Age 12
Bnos Menachem, New York, USA

TONIGHT IS SHABBOS

Tonight is Shabbos, don't you know,
I can't wait to feel its glow.

All dressed in my best,
I go to greet the Shabbos Queen with zest.

I light the candles that let us know
That Shabbos day has a special glow.

Shabbos is here, my favourite day,
After a week of work and play.

How could people not light candles?
How could they say no,
When Shabbos has a special glow?

So enjoy the beauty of the holy day,
Because after that it will go away.

But don't worry, it will come back you know,
So we can all enjoy again its special glow.

Menucha Amzalak, Age 10

Beth Rivkah Ladies College
Melbourne, Australia

SHABBOS LIGHT

Shabbos is such a special gift Jews have. It gives you a chance to do *mitzvot*. There is more to Shabbos than keeping it. It's the special thought of your being proud of yourself when you do the Shabbos *mitzvot* of lighting candles, *davening*, making *kiddush*, and having challah. It's the valuable time with your family that's unique to Shabbos. Some people are poor and all they want is money to keep Shabbos. They want a *siddur* to *daven* with. They wish for just enough money to keep Shabbos holy.

What do you feel when you light candles for Shabbos? Do you think about how lucky you are to have G-d to give you a chance to keep this special day and its *mitzvot* and see those beautiful candles dance? Next time you light candles, don't just do it and say "done." Think about it and see what the dancing flames are trying to tell you. They could be saying thank you for something you have done or they could be crying, wanting you to care about our holy Shabbos. Shabbos candles could light up your world like giving someone a smile.

Dalia Paluch, Age 8

Beth Rivkah Ladies College
Melbourne, Australia

> *Shabbos candles could light up your world like giving someone a smile.*

AS THE SUN IS BEGINNING TO LOWER

As the sun is beginning to lower
When the day is almost done
We light the Shabbos candles
Together, everyone

The shining candles
And *kiddush* cup
The house is sparkling
And kids all dressed up

The world around us is dark
And it's hard to see the light
But if we all light up our candles
Then we'll all see
That spark

Dina Greisman, Age 12
Beis Rebbe School
California, USA

THE POWER OF SHABBOS CANDLES

Shabbos candles are all about spreading the light.
They have the strength to light up the night.
They bring *Shalom Bayis* to the house,
They cause peace and harmony to arouse.
When Sara and Rivka, our *Imahos*, would light their candles, Friday night at dark,
They would cause a small, little flame to embark.
It would stay lit until the Shabbos next week,
Only then would the wax leak.
And then they would light the candles once again
And whisper their quiet *tefilla* to *Hashem*.
So let us each light our own candle Friday night,
And fill up the world with loads of light.

Tzivia Osdoba, Age 9
Bnos Menachem
New York, USA

I LIGHT MY SHABBOS CANDLES

Sparkling bright
It's Friday night
I light my Shabbos candles.

I stand beside my mother
While saying the *bracha*
I light my Shabbos candles.
Each light chases the dark
Showing a Jewish spark
I light my Shabbos candles.

Yehudis Rosenthal, Age 8
Beth Rivkah School
Melbourne, Australia

WE LIGHT CANDLES

I watch as my mother glides into the family room, dressed in a flowing white gown. Today she is an angel, in her Shabbos robe. My father has prepared the candlesticks for her. *Ima* strikes a match and, with delicate fingers, lets the wick and flame touch. Together they embrace, flickering along with the wind, along with the Shabbos music in the air. My mother sways back and forth, fervently whispering and praying for us. And with misty eyes, she looks up and wishes us a "Gut Shabbos."

We light candles on Friday night,
And this little spark makes the world bright,
As you close your eyes and say a *bracha*,
You thank *Hashem* for all Your success.
You start lighting when you're three,
And it reminds us of when we'll be free.
When you light your first candle,
You're as happy as can be,
And will help us bring *Moshiach* speedily.
The Rebbe encouraged spreading light
Of Shabbos candles so bright,
Do your part next Friday night
And light the Shabbos candles before twilight.

Sara Cohen, Age 10

Illinois, USA

A LEGACY OF LIGHT
Thalia Hakin ע״ה
שרה בת מזל ~ YARTZEIT 22 TEVES

We publish this entry and forever honor the soul of this Jewish daughter, taken too soon. G-d knew, although we did not, that the words she wrote the day she submitted this entry would be immortalized in this book. Her soul — with Hashem — is a guiding light for every innocent child who prays for a better world, for light and peace.

Thalia Hakin, Age 9
Beth Rivkah Primary
Melbourne, Australia

> When you light up a candle you light up your neshema. And you light up the world And when you light up the world you make it a better place. like for you me and evrybody. Now the world is dark but soon to be bright for us. And mir$$ hashem mashiach will come.
>
> By Thalia hakin
> 3Bk

"When you light up a candle you light up your neshama. And you light up the world. And when you light up the world, you make it a better place, like for you, me, and everybody. Now the world is dark, but soon to be bright for us. And, im yirtzeh Hashem, Mashiach will come."

♪ SONG
LIGHT UP A CANDLE

Melody by Rivka Leah Cylich
Produced by Sam Glaser
The production of this song based on Thalia's words was sponsored by the Seymour Fox Foundation

"Conquering the World with Light"
Painting by Cheina Brami of France in memory of Thalia Hakin A"H

When you light up a candle
You light up your Neshama
You light up the world
And when you light up the world
You make it a better place
Like for you, me and everybody

Now the world, the world is dark
But soon it will be bright for us
Imyirtz Hashem Moshiach will come
(repeat)

Light light up light up a candle
Light light up light up the world
Light light up light up a candle
Light light up light up the world
(repeat)

We're lighting a candle
Lighting our neshamas
We're lighting up the world
And when we light up the world
We make it a better place
For you, me and everybody
(repeat)

Many of the songs in this book can be listened to at www.JewishGirlsUnite.com/songs.

♀ TIME TO REFLECT
THE DIVINE LIGHT

Take a deep breath in
Breathe out slowly
Take another breath in, 1,2,3
Breathe out slowly, 1,2,3,4

Watch your candle dance and shine.
The visible light of your mitzvah is Divine.
Your Shabbos table, *kiddush* cup and challah are illuminated by your Holy Shabbos candle.
Let the Divine light surround you and feel the power of your One More Light.

Picture the holy sparks ignited with every good deed; a smile, a kind word and a blessing.
"Ki Ner Mitzvah V'Torah Or" - "Every mitzvah is a candle and Torah is light."
(Mishlei)

Every mitzvah you do shines a spiritual light in a dark and confusing world.
Soak in the Divine light and feel the joy of your every good deed.

As you absorb the light of your Shabbos candle,
Picture the light of Paradise descending into the world.*
Open your heart to receive the flow of blessings,
Let the Divine light surround you and feel the serenity and peace of Shabbos.

Note:
*G-d removed the light of Paradise when Adam and Eve ate from the Tree of Knowledge and it returns every week when we light candles. When Moshiach comes, the light generated with every mitzvah will be revealed in the world.

♦ TIME TO REFLECT
HASHEM IS MY LIGHT

Close your eyes.
Think about your past week
Think about an emotional struggle that weighs on your heart
Think about any other struggles or worries that you have had
Think about a concern for the future or conflict that made you sad.

Are you tired of the darkness and negativity around you?
Will you fall into despair? Will you succumb to worry and fear?
What is blocking your soul from shining brightly?
Take a moment to focus on what is concealing your light.

Join me as we discover our source of light.
Let us sing, *"Aishes Chayil Mi Yimtza"*
"A Woman of Valor, Who can find?"
Let us praise our faith that has never failed
With our strength and courage, we always prevailed.

Open your eyes and gaze at the radiance of your lit Shabbos candle
Remind yourself, *"Hashem Ory"** (*Psalm 27)
Hashem is my salvation, *Hashem* is my light
He warms the cold and dispels the night.

Let your Shabbos candle help you see
Your enormous power to dispel darkness instantly
Open your eyes to the infinite possibilities each day
Find the hidden light in each person who comes your way.

Breathe in deeply and breathe out
Let your worries and concerns go, let the anxieties and fears go
Take another deep breathe in and a deep breathe out
Let go and let Shabbos enter, let your inner light shine!

❓ QUESTIONS TO CONSIDER

Light a candle every day!

Think of a dark moment when you felt sad or alone:

How can you find the light and infuse it with meaning?

Think of a person whom you find frustrating for any reason:

How can you see the goodness and light in this person?

Share your answers at www.JewishGirlsUnite.com.

Photo credit: Isabella Roberts IRT photography

CHAPTER 6:

Light of Jewish Women Past, Present & Future

In this chapter, you will see that we are all connected. Do you feel a part of something so precious, so old, so deep, so strong? When you light your Shabbos candles, you are connected to Jewish women of the past, Jewish women of the future, and all Jewish girls and women today who are lighting at the same moment in time.

STORY
RECONNECTING TO MY ROOTS

I am blessed to be part of a large, loud and incredibly loving Jewish family. While growing up, I loved the traditions, celebrations and joy that we experienced around our table. I went to Hebrew School and had a Bat Mitzvah — all of which were very important to me.

At 17, I left for college, and my connection to Judaism became less important. I was searching deeply for meaning, belonging, and truth. The rote prayers in Hebrew that I was able to read but not understand, and a lack of relationship with G-d in my Jewish experience, left me desiring something deeper and more personal.

As a Religion and Philosophy major, I loved the exploration, meditation and mindfulness that I experienced through my studies. By the time I turned 21 and graduated from college, I knew I was Jewish but didn't think much about it. With an invitation to co-author a book on Bhutanese art and architecture, I traveled to the Indian Sub-Continent. When I was unable to enter Bhutan due to visa restrictions, I turned my attention to volunteering and eventually spent 10 years as a volunteer in education both in Nepal and in Pakistan. During that time, I had completely lost touch with my Jewish self.

After returning the US, after 33 years abroad, I began working with Nechama and Jewish Girls Unite. Through open conversation and sharing with Nechama, my feeling of Jewish

> *The first time I lit Shabbat candles, I felt a spark ignite in my own soul, too.*

connectedness was rekindled. When Nechama offered me two candlesticks, I was excited to light Shabbat candles (something I hadn't done as a child). The first time I lit Shabbat candles, I felt a spark ignite in my own soul, too. In my mind, I saw images of other women in my family also lighting candles — my mother, grandmothers, and aunts. I felt connected to my roots in a new and more meaningful way and realized that being Jewish is an essential part of who I am.

Each week I look forward to kindling the Shabbat candles and rekindling the light inside me. Candle lighting has reconnected me with my Jewish soul, and it has allowed me to see myself as part of a strong chain of women and girls who bring light into the world each Friday night.

Julie Hintz *is on the JGU Global Leadership Team and the Founding Administrative Coordinator for JGU. She is the proud mother and grandmother of 6 children and a grandson.*

Julie lighting Shabbos candles in her home.

Mama Rera, Mama Susie, Nonny & Mama Fran

THANK YOU FOR THE LOVE, LAUGHTER, STRENGTH AND LIGHT YOU SHINE IN OUR LIVES!

With love from all of us!

Zayda, David, Lisa, Benjamin, Ellen, Julie, Abi'l-Khayr, Thor, Dave, Sam, Ben, Becky, Mike, Tim, Sarah, Dan, Debbie, Stephanie, Becky, Steve, Evan, Emily, Papa Sandy, Diane, Donna, Sam, Gary, Julie, Max, Myles, Ellie, Sam, Hannah, Neil, Wendy, Adam, Alan, Cynthia, Amy, Mark, Cha Cha, Chase, Jimmy, Liam, Robbie, Steve, Scott, Trish, Leela Andy, Rachel, Eli, Reid, Josie

IN LOVING MEMORY OF OUR MOTHER
Lillian Pesha Leah Bat Shaina Resha Lakub OB"M

Shaina & Azriel Yitzchok Lakub, Lillian's parents

Pesha Leah came to Ellis Island in NY with her family on September 10th 1920 on the ship 'Adriatic'. She was 9 years old. They survived WW1 in and around Cupisk, Lithuana where the Germans were fighting with the Russians. She told stories of her family hiding in a foxhole while bullets were flying over their heads.

Pesha Leah's mother Shaina was an excellent baker and was entered in a contest by the Russians to see who was the best baker in the village. The winner would bake for the soldiers and be able to stay in their house. Shaina won the contest and now the family had challah and food to eat.

Pesha Leah told stories of the family hiding in a hay wagon waiting to escape. A soldier came to the wagon with a pitchfork to see if anyone was hiding in the wagon. Another soldier told him that the wagon was already searched, so he walked away. Pesha Leah said the soldier who stopped him was Jewish. He saved them all!

Pesha Leah said when they were on the Adriatic to Ellis Island, they were all singing and dancing with joy. She, along with her mother, Shaina, father, Azriel Yitzchok, grandmother Raizel and her nine siblings weathered a long tumultuous journey from their home in Lithuania to America.

When they arrived, an uncle met them and took them to his home.

The family eventually settled in Chelsea, MA.

In America, when her grandmother gave her an orange, she was incredibly excited because she'd never seen one before. "It was beautiful," she remembers. She also laughs as she thinks about her first encounter with mannequins - "I thought they were real people!"

Pesha Leah became a private nurse and raised four wonderful sons: Robert, Daniel, Leonard and Edward, who became Rabbi Azriel Wasserman o"bm.

When asked what brings her the greatest joy in life, she replied: "My children and grandchildren."

-FROM HER LOVING SONS

Dear Bubby, the flames you lit are still glowing!

Shaina & Raizel Laber at 3 years old

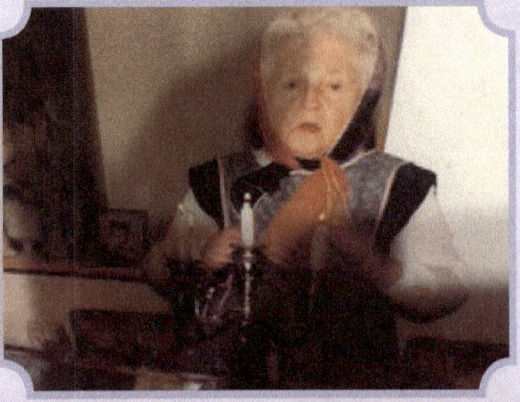

Rivka Laber at Bat Mitzvah

TO THE MATRIARCHS
OF OUR FAMILY

Bubby Rera Schlonsky
& Bubby Gittel Laber

THANK YOU FOR SHARING YOUR LIGHT, LOVE & LAUGHTER FROM GENERATION TO GENERATION.

With Love & Gratitude

Esther Laber, Chicago; Nechama Laber, Troy; Bassie Laber, Miami; Malkie Marrus, S. Antonio; Sorah Leah Eber, S. Diego; Dena Fox, New York; Channi Laber, Miami; Nechama Tauber, Miami; Rochel Laber, Agoura Hills; and families.

Our Pledge

United we stand
Candle in hand
Proud, for it is a legacy
From our mothers to treasure,
to keep, to kindle every week.
Brightening up the night
Bringing a special light
Illuminating the world.
This is our privilege
As women and girls
rekindling souls
the Jewish spark
Bringing the light of Moshiach

♪ SONG
LET'S GET GLOWING

by Chavie Sobel & Racheli Jacks

Let's get glowing
Let's illuminate the night
Light a spark that always stays
Warm and lit and bright

Today let's light a flame
With actions that carry on
Legacies left behind
Outlines that were drawn

Chorus:
JGU, it's in our hands
Together as one we stand
Learning Torah, sharing what we know
Flames that they have lit
We have the power to transmit
For eternity they will glow
Though the night is cold and dark
In our soul, there lies a spark
2x
Girls, light up our world
Let's get glowing now

CHAPTER 6: LIGHT OF JEWISH WOMEN, PAST PRESENT & FUTURE

♪ SONG
LETAKEN OLAM

by Sorah Leah Eber

Looking back over the years
Jewish women prevailed
Brave and modest, bold and kind
Their faith has never failed

From Devorah's wisdom
To Chana's prayer
Esther's self-sacrifice
Rachel's care
Rivka's kindness
And Rivkah's modesty
Leah's gratefulness
Yael's bravery

Jewish women
We have the key
There's much we have to uphold
Using our inner strength from the past
As the future we now mold
They're depending on us to work, to achieve

Igniting the sparks that are left to retrieve
United we stand together as one
Perfecting the world,
Letaken Olam

We may think, just who are we?
This task is way too great
Keep in mind, you're one of a kind
Your strength you can't understate

Just like a midget, though small in size
On giants' shoulders we are tall and wise
Perfecting the world through our nurturing role
With *mitzvos*, with kindness we'll achieve our goal

Chorus:
Jewish women
We have the key
There's much we have to uphold
Using our inner strength from the past
As the future we now mold
They're depending on us to work, to achieve

Igniting the sparks that are left to retrieve
They look down at us
Beseeching us to hear
Their plea to us women
That the future we bear
United we stand together as one
Perfecting the world,
Letaken Olam

Many of the songs in this book can be listened to at www.JewishGirlsUnite.com/songs.

> GLOBAL VOICES

CONNECTING WOMEN FROM GENERATION TO GENERATION

LINKS ON A CHAIN

Surrounded by G-d's presence
Sarah sits waiting;
Finally it's time to ignite the flames
The first link she's creating.
Rivka, Rochel, Leah, our mothers
Continue the chain
Covering their eyes
They silently pray.
They pray for their children
They pray that they'll do right
They pray that they'll continue
The links with their light.

During the Spanish Inquisition
Jewish women hid,
They secretly went to the basement
Where the candles they lit.
They passed on to their children,
Saying to them,
"Remember Shabbos,
A day for closeness with *Hashem*."

During the Holocaust
Women risked their lives,
By kindling flames for Shabbos
Every Friday night.

Up in heaven
There is a chain.
Made by Jewish women
And their Shabbos flames.
Every woman and girl that lights adds a link
That brightens the night.
Soon the day will come
When the world will see
The chain was created
By you and me.
For when *Moshiach* comes,
Every day will be
Like Shabbos
With peace and serenity.

*Up in heaven
There is a chain.
Made by Jewish women
And their Shabbos flames.*

Mushka Heidingsfeld, 14
*Bais Rebbe School
California, USA*

SHABBOS CANDLES

Beginning in New Zealand
The first flame is kindled,
The covered eyes
And whispered prayers
The light is never dwindled.
Continued through Japan,
Russia, England, to name a few,
Every woman
Magical power
Warming the world.
In Alaska
She is the very last one.
She strikes the match gently
Watches the fire flow
Through her home
It spreads the warmth,
Now feel the Shabbos glow.
Her heart explodes in happiness,
A tear rolls down her cheek.
In this chain
Stretched over the globe
She's a very important link.

Mushka Rivkin, Age 13
Bais Rebbe School
California, USA

YOU ARE NOT ALONE

You are not alone
No matter how it may seem
Light a candle
Watch it gleam
Know there is always someone
Who loves you
If you can't think of anyone
I Love You!

Emuna Naiditch, Age 10
Yeshiva Girls School of Pittsburgh
Pennsylvania, USA

A SHABBAT VISITOR

One Shabbat, we had a non-religious guest. She didn't keep Shabbat. When we lit the candles, she saw how beautiful they looked, and how nicely we were dressed, so she started keeping Shabbat. Every once in awhile, she invites us to her house for Shabbat. She lights the candles so carefully and says the *bracha* with such spirit. It is just beautiful!

Shelly Badalov, Age 12
Yeshiva Sha'arei Zion
New York, USA

GLOWING MEMORY

A flick of a match
The glow of a flame
As the candles are lit, a memory pops into the brain.
Six million can no longer be heard
Six million can't share this
sacred light
But they are not
forgotten
They are alive in
every Shabbos
flame.
In every mitzvah
In every prayer
Like an everlasting
ray of sunshine
Their memory shall live on
In the glow of Shabbos candles.

Sarah Dennis, Age 17
iHigh Virtual Academy
California, NY

> *Six million can't share this sacred light But they are not forgotten They are alive in every Shabbos flame.*

THE CHAIN

Everywhere around the world,
On the very same day
Jewish women and girls light Shabbos candles and the blessing they say.

This has been going for years and years,
Sometimes along with many tears.

So when you light the candles,
You're continuing the chain
Created many years ago by women of fame.
Let's go back to Canaan in 2200 BCE,
Jewish women and girls lit Shabbos candles in little cups of tea.

Next to Yemen in the 1200's,
Where they lit with adornments on their heads.

Now to Spain in 1481,
They secretly lit even though it was the Inquisition.

Germany 1939, at the height of World War Two,
Women and girls lit while they wore the yellow star of "Jude."

In our days, there's no need to hide,
So invite a friend and light your candle with pride!

Sara Newman, Age 13
Bais Rebbe
California, USA

CHAPTER 6: LIGHT OF JEWISH WOMEN, PAST PRESENT & FUTURE   135

TWO BEAUTIFUL CANDLESTICKS

I see two beautiful silver candlesticks standing on their tray, ready to be lit. I see my siblings and my mother standing near the candles dressed in their beautiful Shabbos clothing. We are ready to light.

My younger sisters lights first, then it is my turn. I hold the long wooden match carefully in my hand.

After my mother lights, we wave our hands three times and say the blessing. I answer "Amen" as the blessing echoes in my ears. I see the flickering flame of the candles stare at me, so I stare back. I hear the sounds of "Shabbat Shalom" as I give my mother a Shabbos hug. I smell the delicious Shabbos food that my mother and I have baked. We set the table with fancy, shiny silverware. After a relaxing hour, my brother and father walk in as we welcome the Shabbos angels with *Shalom Aleichem*.

Mushky Berghoff, Age 12
Yeshiva Schools of Pittsburgh
New York, USA

MY CANDLE

It's been a long and full week,
My Shabbos candle speaks to me.
"I will reignite your inner flame" —
My candle is lit once again!
My candle is a tiny flame with enormous power,
My candle stays lit all week, just like Sarah's.
My candle is the reflection of Rivkah.
My candle glows in the darkest moments,
My candle is my inner flame that I shine.
My candle will carry me through another week.

Rivkah Laber, Age 12
Maimonides Hebrew Day School
New York, USA

GIVE BACK THE LIGHT

Friday is the epitome of the mundane;
All of the physicality compressed into a day.
But no matter how many renegades reside
in the mortality of this 24-hour day,
I know what is to come once the night falls
Because Friday is also a threshold;
Friday is a passage, a bridge.
No matter how stormy or dry the Friday
afternoon may be,
The sun always seems to set in a golden
pool basked in this holy light
And when the sunset comes,
I am so content with bidding farewell to the
day.

The evening brings upon us a twilight of
candles and matches,
Of oil-filled candelabras.
I light a candle,
Transporting me back in time to Aleppo,
Where my great-grandmother stood
In a war-torn town;
She still covered her eyes,
Saving her deepest prayers for the Creator
Who is always listening.
As I wave my arms in a circular motion,
I am transported to Sunik,
Where my great-grandmother stood
In front of a candlestick belonging to her
great-grandmother,
And although there were blond-haired and
blue-eyed men outside her front stoop in
uniforms
Rounding up her people,
She stood her ground and closed her eyes,
Reciting a blessing that awakens the
compassion in our Heavenly Master's heart.
I await the moment that I can connect flame
to wax, connecting me to my ancestors.

I celebrate in the joy of another week
completed;
Mothers and angels join me in this holy
igniting,
The souls destined to live behind the stones
rise to hear my prayers,
The spirits outside my window peer into
this palace,
These holy beings all witnessing my
connection to this wax wonder;
And I think about its existence before I light
it,
Before I assign it a name, before I make its
creation complete.
This candle is merely a white soldier living
in a box of other troops,
Waiting for the moment where it can
be called upon and therefore worth its
formation.
And even if the room is dim,
With shades drawn, the moment match
births flame,
And wick and fire meet,

The room is enlightened with the glow of the A-lmighty Father sitting in his cloud throne and galaxy Kingdom.

This evening is a drink of cool water to the parched throat,
This day is sustenance to the starving,
This night is new repaired vision to the blind.
And I think to myself,
The least I could do is share this gift with another,
In the hopes they'll recognize its value.
The least I could do is somehow repay the King of the universe for presenting me with such a rarity.
And when my hands cover my face,
When my palms hide the tears that stick to my skin,
I feel complete.

My voice is raised in harmony
For the land I call my home,
For the dove who wishes to return to her nest peacefully,
Carrying an olive branch which she can extend.
I close my eyes and envision a wall whose cracks hold my nation's sorrow within,
I envision a golden city
And hope for its glory to be restored.
The kingdom of Zion has fallen,
And I hope to help lay down the bricks that rebuild it.
My heart holds the Walls and rivers of this nation's land,
And it breaks every time she suffers.

I serve You and Your Torah in the hopes that my beautiful country shall be restored in a holy rejuvenation,
So the least I can do is keep the soldiers in your army in mind.
The least I can do is think of the people giving up their lives so that mine can continue on.
The least I can do is give back.
The least I can do is encourage another to do the same, to take part in sparking another flame.
The least I can do is give back the light He has given to me.

> *The least I can do is give back the light He has given to me.*

Chani Smoller, Age 16
Hebrew Academy of Huntington Beach
California, USA

WHAT SHABBOS CANDLES ARE TO ME

Shabbos candles have always meant a lot to me. After a week of going to school, working, playing, helping, and doing *mitzvos*, for generations, Jewish women and girls would light Shabbos candles and say the blessing. I have always thought that our lighting the candles just the way our *Imahos* did over a thousand years ago, is amazing.

After all the hustle and bustle of the week, we can purify ourselves for the holy Shabbos. Candle lighting is very holy and very spiritual to all, and for Jewish women, it has always held a special place in our hearts.

I was born on Chanukah, the festival of lights, and have always been inspired by the beauty of the bright lights and the spirituality of the blessings on our menorahs and Shabbos candles. I received a candlestick when I was three and was proud to light it with my mother. The next night I lit the menorah with my father. It was really cool. Since then I have enjoyed lighting candles on Shabbos and *Yom Tov* with my mother and sisters, like all the generations of Jewish women since Sarah *Imeinu* until *Moshiach* comes. May *Moshiach* come soon!

Chana Naiditch, Age 11
Yeshiva Girls School Pittsburgh
Pennsylvania, USA

MY MOST CHERISHED EXPERIENCE

My most cherished candle lighting experience, is when my grandparents join us for Shabbos night.

As the sun begins its golden descent, I usher my mother and grandmother to a side table, where I had lovingly set up the Shabbos candles earlier.

As soon as I cover my eyes and recite the *bracha*, I feel deeply inspired and close to *Hashem*.

I share with Him my personal *tefillos*, and an incomparable feeling of calmness envelops me.

I know *Hashem* has heard my *tefillos* as I draw my hands away from my eyes, and that contributes towards my content, Shabbos-enhanced feelings.

But, as I kiss my *Ima* and *Bubby* Good Shabbos, it is like nothing else to stand back to admire the lights kindled by three generations, and to stand beside these beloved women as I, *Baruch Hashem*, am so privileged to do.

Tzipporah Prottas, Age 14
Homeschool
Connecticut, USA

HIDDEN

Two shining flames
Tucked away, hidden
Behind the musty walls
I remain
Immovable
I stand
As the flames
Flicker and dance
I cradle my child
Whispering
Gently in her ear
My dear child
When you grow up
Do not forget
To light these very candlesticks
Remember the Shabbos
My little one
You are a
Jew

Fourteen years go by……

A box
Brown, tied with twine
Inside lies a secret
That can only be mine
I open it with trepidation
Inside amidst tattered fabric
To my elation

Two tarnished candlesticks
Memories awash in my mind
Flames flickering
Somewhere dark and damp
Mama hugging me
Whispering
Do not forget…
Do not forget…
And then
Blank
Perplexed
I steadily make my way
Out of the airless attic
I grab a cloth
Eager
Shining the candlesticks
Hoping to reveal
More memories

Ten years go by……

The sun is setting
In the ruby-coloured sky
I strike the match
Once, twice
A spark bursts forth
I circle my hands not once but thrice
Covering my eyes
Whispering a *tefilla* to Hashem

The flames flicker and dance
As I stand
Immovable
Arms around
My children
I smile
Thinking of my family
Mama would be proud

Rivkale Pink, Age 13
Lubavitch Senior Girls School
Solihull, West Midlands, England

A QUEEN

She stood there
Tall, proud and regal
With righteousness that befits
A queen

This had to be what it felt like
To stand in the presence of
A queen

She stood
Her eyes covered
Before the warm glow
Of the candles
Lit by
A queen

She whispered quietly
Asking
That they should be happy
Those children of
A queen

Then she lowered her hands and
Walked, tall and proud
To hold tight this child,
This loving daughter of
A queen

Emmy Simon, Age 13
Shearim Torah High School
Arizona, USA

LIGHT A SPIRITUAL CANDLE

Jewish females light Shabbat candles from when they are three years old, every Friday evening at sundown.

We can light our candles, not only on Friday, but every day of the week, just like Sarah *Imeinu*. It does not mean we light a physical candle every night. We can light spiritually.

What does it mean to have a spiritual candle lit? It means that every single one of our actions can light up our home, or wherever we are.

When we light Shabbat candles, we are closest to G-d. We can ask for whatever we need. Our prayers will be answered.

My grandmother, my mother, and my aunt's photograph were on the *neshek* brochure in the 1990's. I hope to follow in their footsteps, and shine the light of Shabbat candles all around the world!

Shayna Batya Malamud, Age 10
New York, USA

SHINING BEAUTY

A girl of age two walks up to her mother,
Looking longingly at her older brother.
His statement so proud to show that he's a Jew
She thinks, "Why, oh, why can't I be like you?"
I want to have that declaration, that stamp on my face
To show that I too want to embrace Him
My G-d, in my simple young mind
Where is my chance to search and define?
I'm confused and searching
So hard and unwilling
When will I get that badge to show
That I too have love to bestow?
So far away is marriage and devotion,
She wants the chance, she thinks of a notion:
When will I turn three? Then with true liberty
I can welcome you Queen, so pure and holy.
When that day arrives a smile beams across her face,
She rushes up to the candle in pure joy and haste.
Her relatives and family smile at her sweetly,
Just an innocent young child, looking at the candles longingly.
But beyond their imaginations are her thoughts churning
For the time when it will be the end of her yearning.
She takes the match in her hand
Beside her mother she does stand,
Welcoming in the holy day with thoughts and prayer.
Twenty years later she's still doing the same action
With her own child, who awaits her birthday in great anticipation.
From generation to generation the flame is passed on,
To show and signify that we are the true ones.
For years that have passed and other people's morals had a lack,
The women and the chosen people
Have shown all who were evil
That we will always be the ones
To have won the evil inclination
Of our hearts' purification.
Women have the might
To shine their inner light.
Welcome in the holy day now
And be Jewish women proud.

Raizel Lazaroff, Age 13
Texas, USA

SPECIAL SHABBOS

I feel that the time when we are lighting Shabbos candles is the most special time of the week. When we are lighting the Shabbos candles it is a special time to ask *Hashem* for whatever we need. This time feels very spiritual and very holy. When I am lighting Shabbos candles it is as if I am lighting with my grandmothers all the way back, all those generations back to Sarah *Imeinu*.

Shabbos is also a time of rest. Right after we light the Shabbos candles we feel revived from our hard week.

This is also a special mitzvah because this mitzvah is for all Jewish women across the globe. All Jewish women are united at this time. I have decided that this must be a very special mitzvah because Rabbi Menachem Mendel Schneerson, the Lubavitcher Rebbe, appointed this mitzvah as one of the Ten *Mivtzaim*. This mitzvah is performed right after a busy day of work, *Erev Shabbos*. I will now share a very beautiful poem about the Shabbos candles:

As I sit here
My loaded mind is finally clear.
I haven't felt so calm in a while
And all I can help but do is smile.
My family makes me feel so relaxed, there is nowhere else I'd rather be;
At objects in the room I stare
My emotions no longer in an exploding flare
Of hot flames. I look into my mother's eyes,
Now they are filled with joy of a brilliant sky.
Then I look around and see
My siblings talking quietly, their thoughts free;
Shabbos is here,
It's time to rest and have no fear.

Simi Davidson, Age 12
Yeshiva Schools of Pittsburgh
Pennsylvania, USA

I THINK OF MY SAFTA WHEN LIGHTING CANDLES

I had a *Safta* Sabina who lived in Dzialoszyce, Poland. She died almost two years ago — she was 100 years old. She was a sweet, nice lady and a nice gift from *Hashem*. I think of her a lot, and I feel she is still with us everywhere.

When *Safta* was about 24 years old, before she was married, World War II started and the Germans were headed to Poland. The family was very scared and worried. The three daughters and everyone else in the house were running to hide all of their valuables like jewelry and silverware. They buried the items under coal in the cellar, and they all went to hide in the forest. Then the German soldiers attacked and broke all the windows, and ripped down the houses, and knocked down buildings. My *Safta* ran away to the Russian side of Poland. She met my *Sabba* there, and they got married during the war. Then the Russians sent her to Uzbekistan and she had a baby, my father Arie.

When the war was finally over, five years later, my *Safta*, who was the only one alive, went back to the house to find the valuables. Deep in the cellar she dug with a shovel, finally finding one of the two candelabras. And now my family has it! We light it every Shabbat, and I think of my *Safta* and my whole family.

The candelabra is silver-plated and has five branches. My mother lights a candle for each of us, and I light the one on the very top and center of the menorah.

I think that this is a very nice and special story — and hope it will encourage more Jewish girls and women to light Shabbat candles.

Shoshana Ferber, Age 11
Homeschool
Connecticut, USA

CHERISHING THE MITZVAH

As the sun goes down we start the holy Shabbos by lighting the Shabbos candles. As they flicker in the night, it almost seems that they are telling the story of the *parsha* or the *haftorah*.

They are the perfect dancers, twirling in the night.

> They are the perfect dancers, twirling in the night.

As I gaze at the candles shining so bright, I think of the great women lighting throughout the ages. They lit in the hard times, even when they struggled. They kept their spirits high with Shabbos candles.

Sometimes they lit with tears in their eyes, wishing to live through the week to be able to light the Shabbos lights again. As their husbands sang *zemirot*, they watched the candles with hope in their eyes, praying for this happiness every day.

I am inspired today by their spirit to overcome the darkness with light. I will cherish the mitzvah and continue to shine the light of those women who sacrificed for us.

Musya Presman, Age 11
Yeshiva Girls School of Pittsburgh
Pennsylvania, USA

A NEW FAMILY FOR SHABBOS

Sarah thought of the nights when she observed Jewish families happily lighting candles and enjoying feasts together on Fridays. How she wished to join them, leaving these hard times behind. Sarah had faint memories of being with her parents, celebrating all the Jewish holidays, especially Shabbos, but that was all a very long time ago.

Sarah and eleven other girls lived in a non-Jewish orphanage. The matron, Ms. Smith, was meeting with a woman considering adoption. Ms. Smith left the girls in the schoolroom while she was "doing other business." The children waited, wondering what exactly Ms. Smith was doing.

Finally, Ms. Smith walked in with another woman and announced, "Girls, this is Mrs. Markovich." After a couple of silent seconds, the women turned their backs to the girls and whispered. Then they walked into Ms. Smith's office, leaving the girls wondering what happened. "Oh, and Sarah, come with us."

One week later, Sarah had already joined the Markovich family. It was Friday afternoon and Mrs. Markovich was hurrying around the house, cleaning and getting ready for Shabbos. Sunset came around. After what felt like thousands of years in the orphanage, Sarah lit her candle, feeling so close to *Hashem*, thanking Him for being adopted by a loving family, keeping the traditions of her past childhood.

Shirin Kaye, Age 12
The Philadelphia School
Pennsylvania, USA

ⓘ TIME TO REFLECT
YOUR PRECIOUS LEGACY

Picture our Matriarch Sarah lighting her Shabbos candles in her open tent filled with light, goodness, and peace. Her candles would miraculously burn from one Friday to the next and created warmth and light for her guests all week.

Picture Rivkah lighting her candles in Sarah's dark tent. Rivkah's candles kept the flame of Sarah burning for the entire week once again.

Picture Rachel and Leah kindling their oil-lamps before sunset, laying the foundation of our nation in the golden chain that began with Sarah *Imeinu*.

Picture mothers and daughters lighting candles in the darkest moments of our history, their little flames beacons of light in a dark and gloomy world.

Picture your great-grandmothers lighting Shabbos candles in their humble homes.

Their flames are still glowing...

Now it is your turn. You join their mission to dispel the darkness. Light your candle.

Picture your flame joining their flames. Together, you have more power to light up the world.

Think of one woman whose soul is with *Hashem* above.

What mitzvah did she cherish? What was her unique light?

Picture her performing this mitzvah in her special way. This is her legacy.

What can you do to emulate her goodness?

How will you add one more light in her merit?

Picture her glowing smile.

Feel her bright soul join your soul.

Feel her love and light surround you.

Dear daughter: You carry on her precious legacy! **Her flames are still glowing through YOU.**

AFFIRMATION

I am a strong link in the golden chain of great Jewish women lighting up the world!
I have the power.
It's been given to me.
It is up to me!

❓ QUESTIONS TO CONSIDER

Can you think of one woman in our past whom you want to connect with when you light Shabbos candles this week?

"Sarah and Rivkah's candles openly illuminated the home with a physical light for the whole week*. Yet, the inner effect of women lighting today is the same. The illumination from the mitzvah of our Shabbos lighting influences our whole week. Sarah represents every mother and Rivkah represents every daughter, who inherit the wondrous power of illuminating the home for the entire week through candle lighting." — The Rebbe

How do you keep the influence of the candles shining throughout the week?

When we strive to create an atmosphere of light, love, joy, holiness, and warmth in every corner of our home, the Shabbos candles glow every minute, every hour, every day for the entire week.

If you think: "Who am I to shine and make this world a brighter place?" remember that our Mother Rivkah was only three years old when she began to light candles.

Share your answers at www.JewishGirlsUnite.com.

---

*Did you know?
Avraham lit the Shabbos candles after Sarah's passing but his candles did not last all week. It was only the candles of Sarah and Rivkah that stayed lit all week. This is the power of Jewish women and girls.

CHAPTER 7:
Light of Peace & Redemption

In this chapter, you will learn what redemption actually means! Do you yearn to be free, to break free of the ties that bind you to a mundane existence... the ties that bind you to negative feelings? In the act of lighting your Shabbos candles, you can find a moment of peace, your moment of redemption. Freedom! You are free from the strife of the week, free from your fears, free from whatever overwhelms you in life... even just for a moment. When you light every week, and you find that soul connection every week, you will be in the habit of feeling redeemed... connected, free, joyous!

STORY
MY PERSONAL REDEMPTION

When I was growing up, achievement was redemption. Life was presented as a game. Winning meant having the best job, earning top pay. Realizing those goals required working 24 hours a day, seven days a week. Rest was a privilege that lazy people afforded themselves at the high-pressure high school I attended. At an assembly, the principal told us, "You are the future leaders of the world." And he was right: many presidents, business moguls, and other powerful figures had graduated from my alma mater. Our teachers assigned more homework than we could complete so we would learn how to prioritize.

It felt dangerous to let go of my responsibilities for an entire day.

I operated on overdrive, pulling countless all-nighters throughout high school and college, until a friend of mine invited me to spend Shabbos with her family in New Jersey. The aroma of chicken soup filled the kitchen, making my stomach rumble. My friend and I snuck pieces of fresh potato kugel before getting ready for Shabbos. She and her siblings rushed to meet the deadline, but this time it wasn't for work or school. They needed to be ready for candle lighting. I wasn't used to having a time when all electronic contact would stop. I was afraid to miss an important email for my internship. I didn't want to put aside my paper for 25 hours. It felt dangerous to let go of my responsibilities for an entire day.

Tall silver candlesticks were set in the middle of the table. There was a tea candle set out for me. The room was whisper-quiet as we lit the matches, covered our eyes, and prayed. "Good Shabbos," my friend's mother said as she gently put her hand on my shoulder. The once-bustling household grew calm, peaceful. I had never experienced serenity like that before. I heard my phone buzz, and my shoulders tensed. Until I realized I had entered a new phase of time called Shabbos.

The tiny flame of my candle flickered on the table and I let go of my week, my work, all the stress I carried. And allowed myself to make room for *Hashem*. Soon I began to light my own Shabbos candles every week. I still graduated college with honors, even as I spent 25 hours focused on spiritual connection instead of my homework.

After college, I relished the freedom I felt every Friday night. It felt redemptive to let go of the stress and pressure of my hi-tech job. I had no idea that learning to leave the rush of work behind, along with the single-minded focus on making money and acquiring more material things on Shabbos, would help me in any other way. But when I lost my job in the World Trade Center shortly before 9/11, I was grateful to have a deeper dimension to my life, a vision of light and sense of my purpose in the world..

Yedida Wolfe *is the mother of Sarah, Estee, Leah (and Asher), a writer and Writing Coach for JGU.*

Yedida's daughters lighting Shabbos candles.

GOLD PAGE

IN MEMORY OF
Savta Nesia

AND MY TWO MOTHERS:
Frieda
MY BIRTH MOTHER,
& Eva
WHO NURTURED ME INTO ADULTHOOD.

—NESIA BRENNER

Savta Nesia

Eva

Frieda

Thank you to the incredible Labers! With their help beginning in 1997, our family of six became observant. We personally guarantee you will have fun, as they help you ensure that Judaism will continue as more than just the name of your religion!

With love from the Hertzberg Family
of Pittsburgh, PA, formerly of Clifton Park, NY

To our dearest nieces and cousins
~ Lisa, Simone, Morgan, Meirah, Sivan and Lielle ~
May the gift of lighting Shabbos candles each week shine bright within you for eternity.
Mazal Tov, Sivan on your Bat Mitzvah
We love you,

THE KIRSHON FAMILY

In honor of our dear parents

AVRAHAM C.Y. & ROSE RAPPAPORT

who were among the first supporters of Mivtza Neshek

From Chanie & Rabbi Yaakov T. Rapoport & Family
Shluchim of the Rebbe in Syracuse, NY

In honor of my teachers:
Rebbetzins Nechama Laber, Maryashi Sternberg, Yehudis Wolvovsky, and Rabbi Yosef Resnick
— great leaders of our generation. With their guidance and light, they are igniting sparks everywhere.

LOVE, TZIPPORAH PROTTAS

In celebration of your inner glow,

NECHAMA LABER & SUSAN AXELROD

Love,
Yaffah and Shoshana Ferber

IN HONOR OF
MRS. ESTHER STERNBERG
FROM
LOREN LICHTENSTEIN & FAMILY

I attribute my strengths and inner light to my beautiful Matriarch Leah Chava and my grand-mothers. Rochel, Geula, Miriam and Yocheved. Let their legacy shine through our Shabbos candles. Thanks for passing on the torch and our Torah.

-ARIELLA SAPOZNIK

CELEBRATING JGU - WITH GRATITUDE
Elephantheart.net

MAMAN, MÉMÉ ADORÉE
93 Years from Constantine to Jerusalem
Mémé Rachel Allouche Bouskila ז״ל

1 CHESHVAN - 7 SHEVAT

A su transmettre les valeurs ancestrales juives en allumant ses veilleuses de chabbat priant toujours que la présence divine protège sa famille bien-aimée.

Rachel bat Shalom is buried in Jerusalem, Israel near her illustrious great-grandfather, Sidi Bahi Eliyahu Allouche, the Chief Rabbi and Dayan of Constantine (Algeria).

She communicated her tremendous love for us with her open heart, songs, smiles and laughter, (even though we didn't all understand French).

She inspired us to talk to Hashem and say, "D-ieu aide moi! (G-d help me)" in every situation we found ourselves.

She would put aside some of her delicious baked goods for unexpected guests and say, "Cache pour demain (Hide some for tomorrow)."

Mémé, we miss you, we pray to see your smiling face very soon with the coming of Moshiach.

With Love,

FROM YOUR CHILDREN
PIERRE, DANIELLA, MARTINE,
GRANDCHILDREN AND
GREAT-GRANDCHILDREN

♪ SONG
ANI MAAMIN
by Rivka Leah Cylich

I don't want to play and sing this prayer
I just want to live Your song
A million years of asking
A million years too long

I don't want to close my eyes and dream
I want it here, I want it real
I want to touch it, I want to feel

To see the oneness
Feel the peace
The truth that's blowing in the breeze

Chorus:
Ani Maamin Be'emuna, Shleimah
Be-vi-at Hamashiach
Ani Maamin, Ani Maamin
Ve-af Al Pi Sheyitmahme-ah
Im Kol Zeh Achakeh Loh
Achake Loh, Achakeh Loh
Bechol Yom Sheyavo

(I believe with complete faith
In the coming of the Messiah
And even though he may tarry
Nevertheless I wait each day for his coming*)

*Source: The twelfth of Rambam's Thirteen Principles of Jewish faith

CHAPTER 7: LIGHT OF PEACE & REDEMPTION   155

♪ SONG
MY LIGHTS

by Rivkah Krinsky

I've seen my lights in a place called California
I've seen my lights down under in Australia
I've seen my lights around the world dancing pretty
I've seen my lights crying out through your history

There's a light so pure and so golden
You know the flame in your heart that you're holdin'
Yeah, that flame can burn away the darkness
Shinin' like souls of the righteous

Chorus:
Im atem meshamerim nerot shel Shabbat
*Ani mareh lachem nerot shel Tzion**
Im atem meshamerim nerot shel Shabbat
I will show you the lights of Zion

I've seen my lights from Beijing to Cincinnati
From London to Brazil and Kentucky
From the streets of Russia cold and wintry
But I want to see the lights of my Holy City

At dawn, Jerusalem she cries
Just waiting for the sun to rise
Millions of flames now dancing all together
Let's brighten up this dark world forever

Before the sun sets on your Friday night
Let your light shine onto me
Before the sun sets on your Friday night
Come and share your flame with me

Will you let your light shine down on me?
Will you let your love shine down on me?

Im atem meshamerim nerot shel Shabbat
*Ani mareh lachem nerot shel Tzion.**

*If you will observe the kindling of the Shabbat lights, You will merit to see the lights of Zion.

Many of the songs in this book can be listened to at www.JewishGirlsUnite.com/songs.

💬 GLOBAL VOICES
THE PEACE AND SERENITY OF SHABBOS

SHABBOS PEACE

We may not be in time, we fear,
Our hectic home is filled with stress;
"Quick, cook that soup! Quick, clean that mess!"
We chop the onions, sweep the floor,
And yet, there's always something more.
Somehow, though, it all gets done,
The jobs are finished one by one.
The time comes, we give one last mix,
Put candles in the candlesticks.
We light a match and heave a sigh,
We touch the wicks,
The flames leap high.
We make three circles as flames rise,
Then bring our hands up to our eyes.
We say the bracha for the light,
Ushering in the Shabbos night.
When we remove our hands, the flurry,
The hustle and bustle, the stress, the hurry,
Are gone, with a feeling of peace in its place.
A pure joy is shining on everyone's face.
Now we can rest from the long week;
At last
Shabbos has arrived and the weekdays are past.
At last we have come to Shabbos's start,
And the light of the candles shines in each heart.

Sarah W., Age 14
Homeschool
Michigan, USA

MY CANDLE

I see my candle glowing bright,
As it shines so brightly through the night.

Then I wave my hands 1, 2, 3
And make the *bracha* so beautifully.

Wow, my candle is shining so bright,
It is making a big light.

Hashem will hear my prayer most definitely,
And make *Moshiach* come so speedily.

Chaya Mushka Kievman, Age 14
Beth Rivkah Ladies College
Melbourne, Australia

DANCING IN THE NIGHT

I'm scared as I see
What the blizzard did to me
Fear and Hate
As harshness awaits
Slowly as the sun melts away
From me
The darkness overtook me
Like the shadow of my mourning heart
Struck by lightning, shivering in fright
As I saw the Gan Eden emerald city of light
Feeling united as the Shabbos
Candles glow
Everything is a flow
The stars, the moon, the sun, the home

I'm beaming in the twilight
As I know Redemption will come once again

As the light will redeem us all
In *Yerushalayim, B'ezrat Hashem*
I'll see my family and friends
Smiling at me
In Jerusalem we will be
Holding hands and arms held tight
We will be shining beautifully in the light
As we are happy to be dancing in the night

Malkie Peiser, Age 16
Margolin Hebrew Academy
Tennessee, USA

MY TRUE INNER LIGHT

Peace? Calm? Spiritual freedom? Such big words. How is this reachable? There are so many problems in the world. Each person feels they have the solution to it all. But what if as individuals we can find the calm in ourselves? Why work on settling the world around us when we can settle our hearts?

For years I lived to try to fix everyone else. Each time I faced negativity, I fought. Each time, I battled. And sometimes I thought I won. Yet, the negativity around never eased.

I remember one Friday afternoon. It was right after lighting my Shabbos candle on a cold winter day in tenth grade. The weeks and months that had passed felt long. Cold and long. Cold from spiritual coldness, and long from trying to pull through all that coldness. I had found myself in surroundings where it felt like a challenge to stick up for what I knew was right. I felt a struggle to keep to my standards. I felt I was battling to be who I truly am: A Jewish princess. I let the outside voices into me, and I found myself fighting chaos around.

I gazed at my lit candle. I smiled. I felt it was mirroring me. The true me. The me that wasn't fighting. The me that wasn't facing anything. Just me. The perfect untouched me. I saw my flame. I saw me.

It was so beautiful. It told me I'm beautiful. It told me I'm strong. A candle. A tea light. So simple, yet so complete. Too complete to describe in words. It brought me to inner calm and peace. True peace. Peace from within. So that no matter what went on around me, I had the strength to not be affected. My candle kept me strong.

Each week I light my flame again. Each week I am reminded of who I am. Each time I light my candle, I get the strength for the week ahead. So whenever challenge hits, I know I can always think back to my light - My true inner light.

> *Each week I am reminded of who I am.*

Racheli Dubov, Age 18
Machon Shoshana
Brooklyn, NY

THE SHABBOS ANGELS

We sat and sang
Around the fire
Orange glow
In black of night,

We didn't need
The stars to shine;
Our eyes were lit
Up, clear and bright.

They shone of dreams
Despite the darkness,
Hope and faith
Despite the fear,

And as we sang
There, something stirred, we
Felt a sense
That good was near.

We sat and sang
Around the fire,
Freedom glowed
In black of night

We sat and sang
In spite of dark
There was a sense
That all was right.

B.L., Age 16
Bais Rivkah, New York, USA

ONE LIGHT!

The amazing light flashes through the window for all guests to see
Just like a lit candle standing straight before me.
But it is a great light for everyone to see
Even at fifty years, even at three!
It's an amazing light that shoots straight up to the sky lighting the trees all around us...
Little butterflies with bright orange wings fluttering from place to place plucking yummy nectar from red Roses waiting for the Shabbos Queen to arrive.
This little candle that spreads so much light holds a beautiful fiery flame
Every Friday night thousands of Jewish women and girls starting from the tender age of three all light Their Shabbos candles which unite them as one with one big light together...
Women and girls welcoming the Shabbos Queen can change the world as one big nation
Together as one
With one goal...
To make the Rebbe proud
To inspire others to do the same!
ONE MORE LIGHT!

Chana Friedman, Age 12
Yeshiva Schools of Pittsburgh
Pennsylvania, USA

THE GUIDING LIGHT

The Markstein family had been hiding from the Germans for the past four years. Rachel Markstein, a thirteen-year-old girl, hardly remembered life before the war. The one thing she could recall was the Shabbos candles her mother lit every Friday night. Occasionally, they acquired a match and candle. Then her mother would light it in honor of Shabbos. That is how they lived in the war years. However, little did the Markstein family know that a German soldier found out that three Jews were hiding in a cellar.

"Rachel, stand beside me as I light the Shabbos candle," Mrs Markstein instructed her daughter. As Rachel's mother prayed with her hands covering her eyes, Rachel realized that something was wrong. Her father wasn't home yet, and he had promised to be back a half hour ago. He stressed the fact so much that he needed to be home to watch his wife light the Shabbos candles. Rachel and her mother stared at the candle, mesmerized by its dancing flames.

There was a quiet knock on the door. Mother and daughter started. "It must be Father," Rachel said. Mrs. Markstein opened the door to let her husband come inside. Rachel looked, and looked again. Her father was pale and half of his beard was unevenly cut off. "What happened, Papa??" Rachel cried.

Mr. Markstein looked at his wife, and in a weak voice he began to explain. "As you both know, I was outside looking for food for Shabbos. After I had collected enough, I was heading home, and then, a German soldier came out of nowhere and ripped off half of my beard. Thank G-d he didn't kill me! I don't know if he knows where we are, but on Shabbos I refuse to escape from here. Now let us begin our Shabbos prayers."

Rachel looked at the dancing candle flame, and began to remember the Friday night before the war began. Her mother lit Shabbos candles. The table was beautifully set with a crisp white tablecloth. Two golden braided challahs were laid on the middle of the table. Two silver candlesticks stood at the side of the table. On top of them stood tall white candles; the flames danced then the same way the flame did now.

"Crash. Boom. Crash." Rachel felt the ceiling crumbling over her. She gasped in surprise and shock, and saw one German soldier standing over her father. "My fellow brother, I was the one who tore your beard. Wake up your wife and daughter now!!" The German soldier said in a soft voice. Rachel sat up, as did her mother. "Pack up your belongings, and let's hurry, fast!" the German soldier said.

"Please explain yourself!" Mr. Markstein said. "We have no time — you have to run," the German said. "We must leave now!" he insisted.

Mrs. Markstein quickly wrapped up their belongings in a sheet and tied the ends into a knot. Rachel took their food, and off they went, deep into the forest.

After three hours of walking the German began to explain, "I am a Jew myself, but I don't remember anything about my parents. When I got the command to kill all of you, I listened. I ripped your beard only because my commander was watching. The sight of a Jew, and later tonight, a small candle burning, stirred up memories from deep inside me. I remembered that when I was a boy of three years old I was watching the dancing flame of two candles. Then someone carried me away."

Mrs. Markstein turned to her husband and whispered, "Could this be..?"

"Is this..."

"Is this Levi, our son?"

"It seems possible...I have seen a scar on his left knuckles, in the exact same place that our son Levi had."

"Levi?" The soldier sharply turned his head, his eyes round.

"Yes?" he whispered

"It is you, our son!" Mr. Markstein cried.

Mrs. Markstein hugged him, and cried. "Thank you, *Hashem*, for reuniting us."

Rachel stood on the side, and said, "I never knew I had a brother..."

Rachel looked at the dancing candle flame, and began to remember the Friday night before the war began.

* * *

Levi led his family to a deserted barn. Inside they found food and water. Levi instructed them to ration the food because they didn't know how long they would have to stay there.

Months passed, and finally the war ended.

Levi rejoined his family, and at last, they came out of their hideout. Everybody stood there, just drinking in the fresh air and blinking in the bright sunlight, reveling in freedom.

After a whispered conference with his father, Levi announced to his family, "None of us want to stay in this cursed Poland a minute longer. I have obtained all necessary papers, and next month, G-d willing, we shall leave to Palestine."

Mrs. Markstein embraced Levi. "Levi, Thank you so much for saving our lives! You are so unbelievable!" Rachel added, "It's truly amazing how *Hashem's* hand brought us together through one little candle."

* * *

On a snowy Friday night, around a large wooden table sit twelve people. Rachel's whole family is celebrating 30 years since the end of the war. In a clear voice she explains to the six children gathered there why this is such a special day. You hear her say in an awed whisper to her parents, husband, Levi and his wife, and all the kids, "Only through our family's keeping the tradition, and lighting Shabbos candles at all costs, did we gain our salvation. Through them, Uncle Levi found our family, and he was G-d's messenger to save us. Thank you, *Hashem*, for sending this one candle as a guiding light for us in this dark exile."

Devorah Davydov, Age 12
New England Hebrew Academy
Massachusetts, USA

A BEAUTIFUL, FLICKERING FLAME

Every Shabbos after I light candles, I look at them. The candles have a special meaning to me. They mean peace. The hard week is done. Now we can relax.

The candlelight shines down on me.
It makes me want Shabbos to last forever.

When Shabbos ends, I feel the familiar feeling back and I can't wait for next Shabbos to come.

Chana Block, Age 13
Beth Rivkah Ladies College
Melbourne, Australia

THE SHABBOS FEELING

Every Shabbos after I light candles, I look at them. The candles have a special meaning to me. They mean peace. The hard week is done. Now we can relax.

The candlelight shines down on me.
It makes me want Shabbos to last forever.

When Shabbos ends, I feel the familiar feeling back and I can't wait for next Shabbos to come.

Chana Mandel, Age 10
Gan Yisroel School, New York, USA

Imagine...

A time when all people live in unity,

All nations live in peace;

A time when all of creation recognizes the oneness of G-d.

A world without hunger, sickness or pain.

A world where we are reunited with our loved ones.

A world where Jews gather from the four corners of the world to the Holy Temple in Jerusalem.

A world of true and lasting peace in Israel.

In the merit of righteous women, we were once redeemed from exile in Egypt. So too, it will be in the merit of the righteous women of our generation, and their unwavering belief in the Redemption, that we will be redeemed once again. *(Arizal)*

Your candle ushers in the light of Shabbos into your home and the entire world. In your merit dear Jewish daughter, we will welcome the light of redemption, "The era that is all Sabbath for eternity."

TIME TO REFLECT

A WORLD OF PEACE AND HARMONY

Every Shabbos we envision a world with lasting peace and harmony. A world that will fulfill the purpose of creation. Take time to envision this new reality in your life.

You have all the strength you need to succeed; you are enough; you are cherished for who you are; G-d cares for you in abundance, and you are safe under His watchful eye.

Hashem has chosen this day for you to renew and strengthen your connection with Him, to allow your soul to be at oneness with Him. This is your day to mirror *Hashem's* love for you. It is a time to express your deepest bond through praying, studying G-d's wisdom, and loving others with His infinite love. His unconditional love empowers you to share your love and joy with others.

You radiate joy. You are prepared to bring this joy into everything you do and share it with others.

Visualize the people with whom you want to share your joy. Visualize strengthening your bond with them.

You have G-d's infinite power to light up others. One candle can light hundreds without diminishing its own flame.

You are the candle lighting up others. You are a Lamp Lighter. You give power to the next person to light another flame.

Feel your open hands stretching out to help the poor.

Feel your feet walking with joy to serve others.

Feel your heart calmly beating with love for your family.

Feel your smile radiating warmth to uplift others.

Feel the vibration of your sweet voice praying for those in need.

As you share your joy and strengthen your unity with others, your unity with *Hashem* is also strengthened. *Yo'er Hashem Panav Elecho... Hashem's* light shines upon you.

Your world is now filled with unlimited joy and light.

All this can happen in a moment — it truly can.

All it takes is one small candle. Your one good deed, your one more light, will usher in a time of ultimate peace and harmony forevermore.

**Dear Jewish daughter —
The world is waiting for your
ONE MORE LIGHT!**

QUESTIONS TO CONSIDER

How can you create more peace and harmony in your heart, home and the world?

Share your answers at www.JewishGirlsUnite.com.

GLOSSARY

Heb. Hebrew; Yid. Yiddish; Ashk. Eastern-European pronunciation of Hebrew word; Rus. Russian

Avos Heb. Ashk. Forefathers

Baal Teshuva Heb. A person returning to the practice of Judaism

Bas Mitzvah Heb. Ashk./Bat Mitzvah Heb. A girl who has reached the age (12) of being responsible for keeping the commandments

Bayis Heb. Ashk. House or home

Beis Hamikdash Heb. Ashk. The Temple in Jerusalem

Bentch Yid. To bless

Bracha Heb./Brachos Heb. Ashk. Blessing

Bubby Yid. Grandmother

Chabad Heb. Acronym formed by the first three letters of *Chochmah* (Wisdom), *Bina* (Understanding), and *Daas* (Knowledge). Used also in reference to the Lubavitch Movement.

Challah Heb. Bread made specially for Jewish Sabbath and festivals.

Chassidic Heb. Of, pertaining to, or following Chassidus

Chassidus Heb. Ashk. Movement within Orthodox Judaism founded by Rabbi Yisroel Baal Shem Tov.

Chayus Heb. Ashk. Vigor

Chesed Heb. Kindness

Daven Yid. To pray

Eis Ratzon Heb. Ashk. Auspicious time

Emet Heb. Truth

Emunah Heb. Faith

Eretz Yisroel Heb. Ashk. Land of Israel

Erev Heb. Evening

Gan Eden Heb. Garden of Eden

Geula Heb. Redemption

Golut Heb./Golus Yid. Exile

Gut Yid. Good

Haftorah Heb. A portion of the Prophets read after the weekly Torah Reading.

Hamikdash Heb. The Sanctuary

Hashem Heb. The word used to refer to a name of G-d which is not pronounced; means The Name

Hatzlocho Heb. Ashk. Success

Ima Heb. Mother

Imahos Heb. Ashk. Foremothers

IY"H Heb. Acronym for *im yirtzeh Hashem*, If G-d wills it to be

Imeinu Heb. Our mother

KA"H Yid. Acronym for *kain ayin horah*, Without an evil eye

Kedusha Heb. Holiness

Kiddush Heb. Blessing over wine

Kodesh Heb. Holy

Lehadlik Heb. To light

Lichtalach Yid. Lights / candles

Lubavitch Rus. Name of a town in White Russia. Birthplace of Lubavitch Chassidic Movement

Maarat Hamachpela Heb. Cave of Machpela in Hebron, burial place of *Avos* and *Imahos* Abraham, Isaac, Jacob, Sarah, Rivka, and Leah

Malach Heb. Angel

Menorah Heb. Candelabra

Midrash Heb. Interpretation of Jewish scripture

Mishlei Heb. The book of Proverbs

Mitzvah/Mitzvot Heb. Good deed(s) in a Jewish spiritual context

Mivtzah Heb. Campaign

Mivtzoyim Heb. Ashk. Campaigning

Moshiach Heb. The Messiah

Neiros Heb. Ashk. Plural form of *Ner*, candle

Neshama Heb. Soul

Neshek Heb. Ammunition; can also refer to the acronym for *Neiros Shabbos Kodesh* (Holy Shabbos Candles)

OB"M Acronym for Of Blessed Memory

Parsha Heb. The weekly portion of the Torah

Pushkah Yid. Charity box

Rebbe Yid. A pronunciation of the Hebrew word which means my teacher or mentor; a *tzaddik* (a completely righteous individual) who leads a group of *Chassidim*

Refuah Shelemah Heb. A complete healing

Rosh Hashanah Heb. The New Year

Sabba Heb. Grandfather

Savta Heb. Grandmother

Sephardic Heb. Originally Spanish Jews, but more recently includes Middle Eastern Jews as well

Shabbaton Heb. A retreat taking place over the Sabbath

Shabbos Heb. Ashk. /Shabbat Heb. The Sabbath; the time between sunset on Friday night until dark on Saturday night.

Shalom Heb. Hello, goodbye, and peace

Shalom Bayis Heb. Ashk. Marital harmony

Shamor Heb. Preserve or protect

Shema Heb. A Biblical passage declaring the unity of G-d

Shlucha Heb. Female emissary

Shluchim Heb. Emissaries

Shul Yid. A synagogue

Siddur Heb. A prayer book

Talmud Heb. The collection of Jewish law and tradition consisting of the *Mishnah* and the *Gemara* and being either the edition produced in the land of Israel or the larger, more important one produced in Babylonia.

Tefillin Heb. Small black leather boxes containing Biblical passages including the *Shema*; worn by men every day except the Sabbath and Festivals

Tefilla/Tefillos Heb. Ashk. Prayer(s)

Torah Heb. The written law; the five books of Moses

Tzedekah Heb. Charity; literally, righteousness

Yerushalayim Heb. Jerusalem

Zachor Heb. Remember

Zechus Heb. Ashk. Merit

Zmirot Heb. Jewish religious songs

Zohar Heb. Classical book including the teachings of "Kabbalah"

CANDLE LIGHTING BLESSINGS FOR HOLIDAYS

WHEN LIGHTING CANDLES FOR ROSH HASHANAH:

Ba-ruch A-tah A-do-nai E-lo-hei-nu Me-lech ha-olam a-sher ki-deshanu be-mitz-vo-tav ve-tzi-va-nu le-had-lik ner shel [if Rosh Hashanah falls on Shabbat add: Sha-bat vi-shel] Yom Hazikaron.

Blessed are You, L-rd our G-d, King of the universe, who has sanctified us with His commandments and has commanded us to light the candle of [if Rosh Hashanah falls on Shabbat add: Shabbat and] the Day of Remembrance.

Bo-ruch a-toh Ado-noi E-lo-hei-nu me-lech ho-olom she-he-che-ya-nu vi-kee-yi-ma-nu vi-hi-gee-an-u liz-man ha-zeh.

Blessed are you, L-rd our G-d, King of the universe, who has kept us alive and sustained us and let us reach this time.

WHEN LIGHTING CANDLES FOR YOM KIPPUR:

Ba-ruch A-tah A-do-nai E-lo-hei-nu Me-lech ha-olam a-sher ki-deshanu be-mitz-vo-tav ve-tzi-va-nu le-had-lik ner shel [if Yom Kippur falls on Shabbat add: Sha-bat vi-shel] Yom Ha-Ki-pu-rim.

Blessed are You, L-rd, our G-d, King of the universe, who has sanctified us with His commandments and has commanded us to kindle the light of [if Yom Kippur falls on Shabbat add: Shabbat and] Yom Kippur.

Bo-ruch a-toh Ado-noi E-lo-hei-nu me-lech ho-olom she-he-che-ya-nu vi-kee-yi-ma-nu vi-hi-gee-an-u liz-man ha-zeh.

Blessed are you, L-rd our G-d, King of the universe, who has kept us alive and sustained us and let us reach this time.

WHEN LIGHTING CANDLES FOR SUCCOS, SHAVUOS, AND PASSOVER:

Ba-ruch A-tah A-do-nai E-lo-hei-nu Me-lech ha-olam a-sher ki-deshanu be-mitz-vo-tav ve-tzi-va-nu le-had-lik ner shel [if festival falls on Shabbat add: Sha-bat vi-shel] Yom Tov.

Blessed are you, L-rd our G-d, King of the universe, who has sanctified us with His commandments, and has commanded us to kindle the light of [if Festival falls on Shabbat add: Shabbat and] the Festival Day.

Bo-ruch a-toh Ado-noi E-lo-hei-nu me-lech ho-olom she-he-che-ya-nu vi-kee-yi-ma-nu vi-hi-gee-an-u liz-man ha-zeh.

Blessed are you, L-rd our G-d, King of the universe, who has kept us alive and sustained us and let us reach this time.

ACKNOWLEDGMENTS

"Every blade of grass has its angel that bends over it and whispers, 'Grow, grow.'" -Talmud

No great endeavor happens by a single person. We want to thank the following people for helping to bring this book to light. Each of you is an angel whispering to a Jewish daughter….this book would not be in the hands of generations of Jewish women and girls without you.

We want to start with love and thanks to our husbands, Rabbi Avraham Laber and Dr. Howard Axelrod. With patience, they supported the endless hours over two years while this book was created. Without their loving support, it would have been work; with it, it has been a reward.

- Chaya Yehudis Dank for glossary
- Esther Rosen for the cover artwork
- Mrs. Esther Sternberg, Director of the Candle Lighting Neshek Campaign for over 40 years, for your guidance and encouragement
- Julie Hintz for editing and formatting global voices
- Leah Caras of Carasmatic Design for book design
- Mr. and Mrs. Yehudah and Chana Chakoff for being the first One More Light book underwriters
- Rabbi Avraham Laber for editing and glossary
- Rivka Leah Cylich for composing the JGU Theme songs: 2015 Your Inner Light, 2016 One More Light, 2017 Thalia's Legacy Song
- Sara Leah Eber, Chaviva Elharrar, Chanale Fellig, Rabbi Yitzi & Dina Hurwitz, Jewish Girls Retreat, Rivkah Krinsky, Mali New, and Chavie Sobel for permission to include your beautiful songs about Shabbos and the power of women
- Sarah Greenfield for photography of girls lighting Shabbos candles at the Jewish Girls Retreat
- Susan Axelrod for chapter introductions, for editing and for envisioning this book from conception to production
- 'Time To Reflect' and 'Questions To Consider' written by Nechama Dina Laber with inspiration, contributions and editorial assistance by Susan Axelrod, Rivka Leah Cylich, Julie Hintz, Devorah Leah Schulman and Miriam Yerushalmi
- To all proofreaders: Susan Axelrod, Yehudis Cohen, Chaya Yehudis Dank, Sara Leah Eber, Sofia Muhlmann, Dina Rosenfeld, Chana Shloush and Bluma Weinberg
- To all the schools that submitted their students' entries
- To all who purchased Tribute and Legacy pages, for sharing your loved ones with us
- To our Jewish daughters everywhere, for all time
- To women who submitted stories: Susan Axelrod, Julie Hintz, Nechama Dina Laber, Leah Namdar, Linda Schwartz, Yedida Wolfe and Miriam Yerushalmi
- To *Hashem* for bringing us together

So many were involved in creating this book, we fear that we might have left someone out! If we did, we ask your forgiveness. Please let us know, and we will revise the next edition.

THANK YOU TO ALL SPONSORS OF THE ONE MORE LIGHT CAMPAIGN

Claudia Carral Allouche
Becky & Steve Ast
Charles & Martine Attuil
Susan Axelrod
Daniel Barouk
Diane Blackwell
Nanette & Arthur Brenner
Carasmatic Design
Philip & Linda Chandler
Yehudah & Hannah Chakoff
Stephanie Chesnick
Vanessa Newman Caron
Bonnie Chavin
Ahuvah Coates
Mordechy & Mashi Donat
Racheli Dubov
Sara Leah Eber
Debbie Evans
Chana Feinstein & family
Yaffah & Shoshana Ferber
Moshe & Dena Fox
Deborah Friedson
Leah Gaies
Ricardo Goldschmidt
Leah & Yitzchock Gniwisch
Bruce & Debbie Gross
David Gurevich
Meyer & Shaindy Gutnick
Sara Hecht
Shimon & Sarah Hecht
Yehudis Hecht

Leah Chava Hertzberg & family
Julie Hintz & Abi'l-Khayr & family
Timothy Hintz
Avrohom & Racheli Jacks
Dr. Edward & Laura Jacobs
Donna Jaffe
Neil, Wendy & Adam Jaffe
Sandy Jaffe & family
Tiara Jaron
Jack & Ellen Kaplowitz
Yaacov Katz
Yitzchok & Daniella Katzenberg
Marjorie Kellner
Brian & Carol Kirshon
Shmuli & Mimi Kopfstien
Rachel Kriheli
Yitchok Krimmer
Avraham & Nechama Laber
Shmuel & Gittel Laber
Eli & Rachel Laber
Mayor & Sara Langer
Shoshana Brenenson Libman
Lauren Ferber Lichtenstein
Sam & Rosalynn Malamud
Fanny Miara
Chana Zelda Minkowitz
Rivky Belinov Mishulovin
Rivka Namirovski
Eli Nash
Neshei Chabad of Kansas City
Moishe New

Raizel Roth Nissam
Reeva Novitz
Anita Katz Peiser
Tzipporah Prottas
Chani & Yaakov Rapoport & family
Joseph Rocklin
Mirele Rosenberger
Rachel & Moshe Rosenfeld
The Rosenblum Law Firm, P.C
Yakov & Tzivia Chaya Rosenthal
Ariella & Michael Sapoznik
Rivka Sari
Reva Schlonsky
Dov Schochet
Ory & Linda Schwartz
Seymour Fox Foundation
Rae Shagalov
Mendy & Chaya Shepherd
Rivka Simon
Rachel Loonin Steinerman
Elise Sternlicht
Ellen Stone
Stan & Francine Stone
Menachem & Nechama Tauber
Natalia Thalheim
Daniel Wasserman
Ezzy & Chana Wasserman
Leonard & Andrea Wasserman
Yedida Wolfe
Miriam Yerushalmi
Nechama Dena Zweibel

With apologies, please let us know if we have misspelled or omitted your name.

Our Jewish daughters are lighting up the world!

WWW.JEWISHGIRLSRETREAT.COM

JGU ONLINE PROGRAMS

BEYOND BAT MITZVAH

Unlock the treasures entrusted to Jewish women and girls through a combination of text study, lively discussion and games. We will delve into the lives of women in the Torah and explore related topics and contemporary issues that will guide us in our role as women in modern times. Discover the tools to blossom into a true Bat Mitzvah, a life long goal.

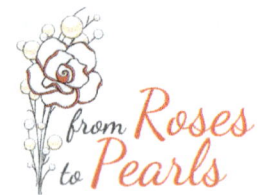

FROM ROSES TO PEARLS WOMEN'S WORKSHOPS

Find joy and meaning in our Jewish holidays and prayers. Discover transformitive tools, tips and meditations from the wisdom of Chassidus. Join a community of women who see through the thorns, smell the roses and transform irritations into pearls.

MIRROR REFLECTIONS FOR TEENS

Join the quest to discover tools and techniques to find your sense of self and achieve inner joy and peace. Using a mirror as a tool for exploration, we will look beyond the mere reflection that is skin deep, share life lessons from Jewish women of our history and focus on a vision for your future that will reveal your inner beauty and strengths today. Integrated throughout the course are life-skills and resume-building opportunities and an integrated opportunity for connecting with other Jewish high school girls from around the country.

JGU EDUCATORS FORUM

Join our free monthly educator's forum, a community dedicated to bringing creativity and innovation into Jewish education. Your students will benefit from inter-school broadcasts and JGU curricula.

CREATIVE ONLINE CLUB

Cultivate your natural talents in art, music, writing and science! Unite with talented Jewish girls from around the world. Discover your Jewish self through the arts. Meet Jewish artists online. Become a JGU Shining Star!

This coupon entitles you to ONE FREE MONTH of online JGU classes.

To register, visit **www.jewishgirlsunite.com**. Email jewishgirlsunite@gmail.com and mention this coupon to redeem. One coupon per person. Only valid for new students.

www.ingramcontent.com/pod-product-compliance
Lightning Source LLC
Chambersburg PA
CBHW060513300426
44112CB00017B/2656